Glimpses of India
Some 5000 Years Ago

A Story of Our Rich Cultural Heritage

Glimpses of India
Some 5000 Years Ago

A Story of Our Rich Cultural Heritage

Rajesh Lal

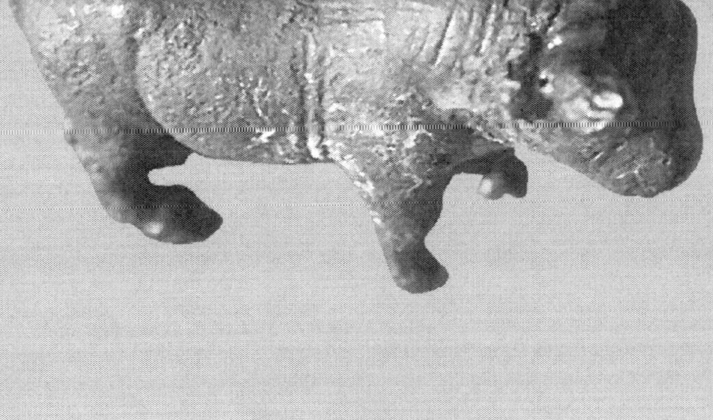

Aryan Books International
New Delhi

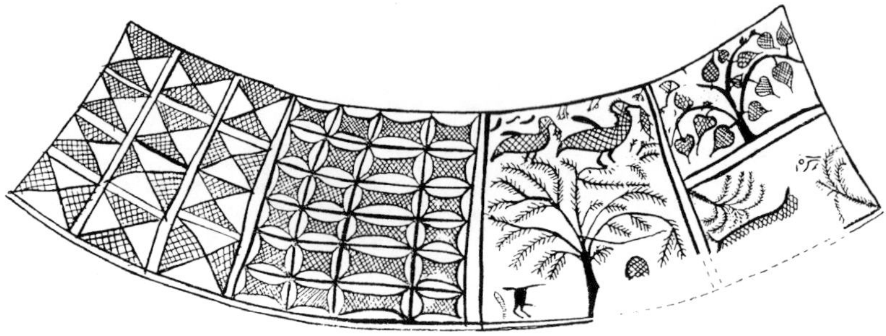

GLIMPSES OF INDIA
Some 5000 Years Ago

ISBN: 978-81-7305-566-9

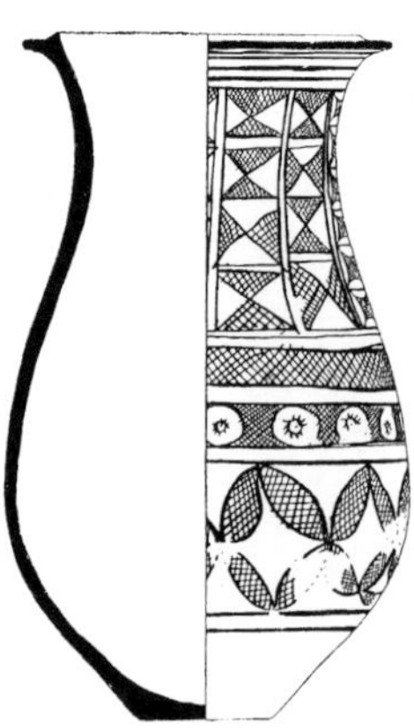

Published in 2017 by
Aryan Books International
Pooja Apartments, 4B, Ansari Road, New Delhi-110 002 (India)
Tel.: 23287589, 23255799; Fax: 91-11-23270385
E-mail: aryanbooks@gmail.com
www.aryanbooks.co.in

Designed and Printed in India by
ABI Prints & Publishing Co., New Delhi.

This book is dedicated to my father

Professor B.B. Lal

The role model and the '*Bhīṣma Pitāmaha*' of the large LAL family and,

I would like to believe, of Indian Archaeology,

And to my mother

Shrimati Kusum Lal

the non-paid 'technical assistant' to Professor Lal,

who accompanied him to *all* his excavations

in India and abroad

Preface

My father, Professor B. B. Lal, retired as the Director General of Archaeological Survey of India in 1972. He had sought premature retirement after serving four years in that position; his age then was 51 years. The assignment that he held did not permit him to pursue his passion of research and excavation. Having been a part of excavations at Harappa, and having conducted excavations at sites connected with the *Mahābhārata,* he had pursued excavations at Kalibangan in Hanumangarh district of Rajasthan to unravel the Indus-Sarasvati Civilisation on the Indian side of the subcontinent. After retiring, he took up excavations at sites connected with the *Rāmāyaṇa*. He wrote extensively to espouse his three passions: that there was no Aryan Invasion or immigration, secondly that the Aryans were actually the Vedic people, and thirdly there is an element of historicity in the epics *Rāmāyaṇa* and *Mahābhārata*. Of all the books that he has written and the theories that he has expounded, there has been a fair acceptance of his arguments and no rebuttals have been forthcoming.

It is his belief that although the books were meant for scholars, their contents would very much appeal to any average reader who would be interested in knowing our heritage. He wanted a publication which you and I could understand easily, and get to know of our ancient culture which is as old as any other in the world. What is more important is that our culture has withstood the test of times and there exists a continuity of our civilisation, which is not so in either the Egyptian or the Mesopotamian context.

He, therefore, was keen that our ancient civilisation, stupendous in its form and rich in content, be presented in the form of a book in such a manner that general public, including school and college going students, get to know about it. It was also necessary to highlight the aspect of continuity of culture that survived the five millennia of our civilisation. He asked me to work on this, and I must state that it is a singular privilege that he trusted me to do this.

This book is based on his and associated writings and it has his blessings!

Contents

Acknowledgements

As a non-student of either history or archaeology, or for that matter any subject associated with our past, it was a brain-scratching exercise when my father, Prof B.B. Lal, asked me to proof-read his books almost fifteen years back. Once I started doing that, I was fascinated by our past. When doing the task that he assigned to me, he was always very patient as he answered my doubts. Thus he had laid a background information, a sort of library in my brain that remained to a large extent a vital 'bank' when I commenced this book. To him, I remain ever indebted for this learning process and also for the values he set in our lives by sheer personal example, that too without a word being spoken. My mother, Shrimati Kusum Lal, even to this day, has enough memories of excavations to give me inputs here and there.

My wife Sushama has been a constant help with any type of assistance required without a care about her own work, which is plenty and requires her time incessantly. My children, Nirupama and Anjali, both in their mid-thirties are ever encouraging on my new venture. To them, I say, huge thanks.

I have read books by some world renowned archaeologists, mention of whom has been made in 'Further Readings', and I thank them profusely. Special mention must be made of Michel Danino for his book, 'The Invasion that Never Was'.

Finally, to my publisher, Mr Vikas Arya, who has been a great help in my first venture, I extend warm thanks.

List of Illustrations

A few illustrations have appeared twice. This has been done to provide ready reference to the reader.

SECTION 1

Our Cultural Heritage

Introduction 1

As late as the first quarter of the twentieth century, it was believed that the country's civilisation was no older than the sixth century BCE and that it had no culture or history that could be dated prior to that century. But in 1921, excavations conducted by Rai Bahadur Daya Ram Sahni at Harappa (see Fig. 1.1) under the auspices of the Archaeological Survey of India opened up pages of Indian culture and history to third millennium BCE. In the following year, 1922, R.D. Banerji opened up the same chapter of our civilisation at another place called Mohenjo-daro. The initial discoveries were sufficient to place this civilisation to an era comparable with Egyptian and Mesopotamian civilisations. Further excavations of these sites reaffirmed the historicity of the civilisation and made the world take recognition of the fact that India did have a civilisation as old as the ones mentioned above. In fact, the area covered by our civilisation exceeds the area covered by both the other civilisations combined.

Harappa and Mohenjo-daro formed the major sites of what came to be known as the Indus Valley Civilisation in the pre-partition days. With the partition in 1947, these sites went to Pakistan with practically no site of that era left on the Indian side.

What emerged in the years following the partition of India was the unfolding of the civilisation contemporary with the Indus Valley Civilisation in the then Sarasvati valley, the present day combine of Sarasvati and Ghaggar in Panjab and Rajasthan, and the same river going by the name of Hakra and Nara in Pakistan. Sixty-five years of exploration and excavation by Indian archaeologists along the then Sarasvati and also in Gujarat have produced a large number of sites dating back to similar era and of the same civilisation. Most notable are Lothal which gave us a dockyard dating back to 2500 BCE, Kalibangan which gave us one and the only excavated ploughed agricultural field in the world and the one and only evidence of an earthquake, both of the same vintage, and Dholavira, the set-up of an ideal city. Text books should now be referring to this civilisation as 'the Indus-Sarasvati Civilisation' and not merely the 'the Indus Civilisation'. There is no justification in using the latter term. This is because the Sarasvati valley is indeed *the centre of gravity of the civilisation* containing so many sites associated with the Harappan Civilisation, with its western limit being the Indus valley. To still call it 'The Indus Valley Civilisation' would be ignorance of post-independence findings through explorations and excavations.

These excavations have shown that our civilisation is ancient, dating back to some five thousand years and our traditions and culture have continued to flourish despite the passage of time. All of it has been brought out so well in the two books by Prof. B.B. Lal, namely, *The Sarasvati Flows On: The Continuity of Indian Culture* (2002) and *How Deep are the Roots of Indian Civilisation? Archaeology Answers* (2009).

The uniqueness of the Indus-Sarasvati Civilisation when compared with those of Egypt and Mesopotamia is that in our civilisation, the rich and poor stayed in singular type of city. There was no differentiation except in the location of their quarters. Indian Civilisation did not have the pyramids of Egypt or the Royal tombs excavated in the Sumerian city of Ur in Mesopotamia. Indus-Sarasvati settlements that have places designated as citadels did not consist of palaces; however, they had large houses to accommodate the rulers, who appeared to be 'the first among the

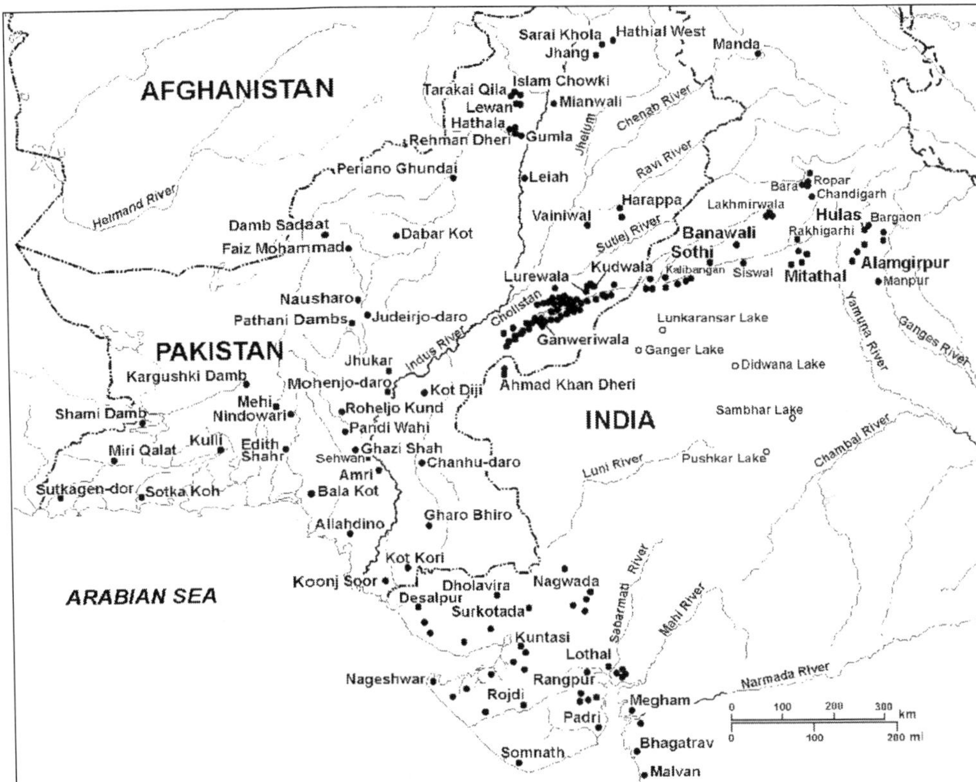

Fig. 1.1. Map of Indus Civilisation.

equals'; the priests, with places of worship, had specific places of residences, and there were residences for the commoners and workers.

The pyramids and tombs do not reflect continuity of their civilisation. But there is something from the same age that reflects continuity in the Indian context. You will see that as we go through a journey of our heritage.

And can there be a more glorious continuity than that the Ṛigveda, which was passed on by word of mouth from the fifth millennium BCE, and was put into text form when we had learnt to write, is still recited by the priesthood! That reflects the continuity of spirituality, a heritage not only of material but of mind, of God.

It will be my effort to bring out this 'continuity' of culture and 'simplicity' that is still prevalent across the large swathes of India in this book.

You must have also realised that despite being ruled by foreign dynasties and colonisers, how we have withstood the onslaughts of body and mind for nearly a thousand years and two centuries respectively of their rule and at the end of it all, came out with our culture and religion intact.

In Section 2 of the book, I have discussed debates related to issues allied to the subject. I have dealt at length on the theories the Britishers espoused when they colonised India. These relate to concept of Indo-Europeans, hijacking of Sanskrit from India to be push-fitted as an Indo-European language, the issues pertaining to the original habitants of this civilisation, the Aryan invasion, and their approach to 'Aryan' and 'Dravidian' race which ended up creating an internal divide in the country, and which still exists.

The reason I felt compelled to do this is: I asked a few 60-year old, a few 50-year old, a few 40-year old and a few 30-year old, such people who were not involved in academics but nonetheless professionals in their respective fields if they believed that the Aryans invaded India? The answer in each case was, "Yes, why do you ask this? Weren't you also taught the same in school?" I felt that I needed to add my bit by telling them through this book that there is another opinion and before our text books are re-oriented, they may like to know the changes taking place in the academic world and make them aware as to how there had been a deliberate attempt to distort the history of India.

To this end, there are five chapters in the section just mentioned. These are *'Decline of Harappan Civilisation and Invalidity of "Aryan Invasion" Theory'*, *'Who were the Inhabitants of the Harappan Civilisation'*, *'Genesis of the Aryan Invasion Theory: A Piece of "Jigsaw" Push-Fitted into the Mosaic of British Rule in India'*, *'Aryan Invasion Theory and Out of India Theory'*, and *'In Conclusion'* where I have posed some questions to the proponents of the 'Aryan Invasion theory'.

Nearly all quotes mentioned in these chapters are by foreign scholars lest one thinks that views of a particular section of Indian society and the way of thinking are being buttressed.

All views and the arguments that I put forward are the result of my own conclusions. I would welcome any sort of feedback to correct myself and enhance my knowledge.

I write as an amateur and am proud of our culture and heritage. I do hope that I have been able to put this across in a simple manner so that 'public at large' will be able to appreciate our history.

2 Archaeology
A Tool to Know Our Past

We know our history because someone, during his time or at a later time, decided that events of that period needed to be recorded for posterity. Great kings wanted the world at large to know how they ruled their kingdoms, how they won territories and expanded their empires. If not they, the official commentators, or the *'prajā'*, the public, would be recording events. Biographies were written on great people, their life events recorded for what they had done for humanity. Epics were born; sages wrote and even recorded what the God's voice told them. Remember all our scriptures were written that way.

But all of the above requires one basic need, one basic ingredient. And what is that?

Of course, a script, a writing system.

What if there is no script, if our ancestors thousands of years ago did not have a method to write things down, and could not leave a record for us to know about that period, since there was no a, b, c....

That period is known as prehistory, a period where there was no script and contemporary writing methods, a period where there is no availability of written records. It is said that 99% of human history is not recorded because it lies in the prehistory period.

What if there did exist a script and we have not been able to decipher it? Well, it is as good as not having any first-hand knowledge of the era.

Here is where archaeology comes to our help. Archaeology is a science and an art, too! It is the study of human activities of the past by firstly surveying a predefined area known to have had a past, then if there exists a strong evidence of what we are looking for by way of discovery of surface materials, then excavating. By means of excavations, ancient buildings below the surface have been discovered along with material culture and artefacts of the era.

Archaeology uses stratigraphy, i.e. each layer of excavated earth signifies a particular period and as we dig deeper, which in fact is the next lower stratum, we go back to earlier periods in time. In other words, successive cultures will emerge in different strata, the ones lower down will be older than those higher. Coupled with C-14 dating, explanation of which is given a little later, we can get to know how old the area under excavation was.

Once excavated, plan-drawing of the entire excavated site is made. Drawings of specific areas are made. What has been discovered and *where* it has been discovered are catalogued. These are then studied and analysed. We shall see all of the above as we go along. The extent of knowledge gained is phenomenal.

Archaeology is not a stand-alone discipline that can sort out all answers to the past. It is assisted in its findings by various other disciplines. For example, Archaeo-botany which would help in identifying the remains of grains, cereals; Archaeo-zoology would assist in identifying remains of animal bones; Anthropology which would assist in giving details of human remains, study of skeletons, *nativity* of remains and other associated issues; physics; chemistry; art history in cases of discovery of cave dwellers and their drawings (there are quite a few which are famous); and others.

Such is the vast array of disciplines that go into deciphering an excavated site with which we get to know our past: how old it was, how the people lived, what they ate, wore, what the culture was like, etc.

Let us take a journey, then, into our past as it existed from fifth millennium BCE till about the beginning of second millennium BCE. But before that, some preliminaries would be in order.

'Ages' Used in Archaeology 3

THREE-AGE SYSTEM

Wikipedia defines the 'Three Age System' in archaeology and physical anthropology as the periodization of human prehistory into three consecutive time periods, named for their respective tool-making technologies. These were the Stone Age, the Bronze Age and the Iron Age. As can be appreciated, the ages may overlap or their start or end may vary by a thousand years or they may vary from region to region. What follows is a generally accepted figure.

THE STONE AGE

The Stone Age can be considered to be divided further into the following ages:

Palaeolithic Stage

Palaeolithic Age is the prehistoric period of human history distinguished by most primitive stone tools. It starts from the earliest known use of stone tools which is said to be around 2.5 million years ago till 12000 BP. (BP stands for Before Present, a term used in geology, datum being 01 January, 1950, and after which radiocarbon dating technique came to be accepted as a tool to determine the age of organic materials.) During this period, humans survived on plants and animals. The age is characterised by use of stone tools. The Palaeolithic means 'old stone age'.

Mesolithic Stage

Mesolithic is a period falling between Palaeolithic and Neolithic ages. Any archaeological material or culture that does not fit into either of the above but falls between the two periods may be termed Mesolithic. It can be placed between 12000 to 7000 BCE.

Neolithic Stage

Neolithic Age is considered to be between 7000-4000 BCE in the context of the mountainous region to the west of the Indus Valley. It has two periods, the later one in which ceramics were used and the earlier one in which ceramics were not known. The aceramic Neolithic can be placed as 7000 to 5500 BCE and the ceramic Neolithic at 5500 to 4000 BCE meshing into the Early Harappan Age. The Neolithic means the 'new stone age'. Mehrgarh in Baluchistan is the most important site of this time. It has been through aceramic, ceramic and copper periods. However, it is not a Harappan site.

BRONZE AGE

The Bronze Age is the second principal period after the Stone Age. In this, bronze was obtained by smelting copper with tin. The result was a hard and a tough metal. The use of bronze in wares and artefacts was so significant, pronounced and prominent that the period was given the name, the 'Bronze Age'. It begins in India around 3500 BCE with the Early Harappan period and continues into the mature stage of the Harappan Civilisation. However, in the period prior to the Bronze Age, copper was used by itself. This period is known as the Copper Age and is considered to be part of Bronze Age. Bronze Age is also characterised by proto-writing, which can be described generally as writing based on symbols. Indus script during that period is an example.

IRON AGE

Iron Age is the last principal period in the Three Age System. It is characterised by societies and culture of that time using iron *and steel* for their cutting tools and weapons. Iron, per se, is not hard, any harder than bronze but when smelted with carbon, it makes steel, and that is an improvement in the toughness over iron and bronze. During this period, the societies graduated from writing in symbols to writing in alphabets. This gave rise to development of languages, writing texts and preserving history as manuscripts.

4 Explanatory Notes on Some Terms

Agate — Agate is finely grained microcrystalline quartz. It is associated with volcanic rocks and is also seen in metamorphic rocks. It is translucent, can be of many bright colours and be of banded variety. It is an inexpensive gemstone and is a very attractive item in jewellery.

C-14 Dating — Carbon-14 (C-14) dating is a method to determine the age of a material that contains carbon which may be as much as 60,000 years old. It is ideal for dating organic materials like plant and animal remains that were found in excavations. The basic principle is that when plant and animals die, they will have a level of the then existing C-14 in their being due to photosynthesis and intake of food materials respectively. In other words, this level of C-14 will be equal to the level of C-14 in the atmosphere at the time when they stopped living. Once that organic material stops receiving the atmospheric C-14, decay in the level starts at a fixed rate. A ratio of what it was and what it is when tested will give the age of the sample. This is a simple explanation, however, there are variables such as the decay of C-14 in atmosphere not being linear, etc., but correction factors are required to be inserted to get to the closest dating.

Carnelian	Carnelian is a variety of silica which gets its dark red colour due to impurities caused by iron oxide, thus giving it a cherry colour. It is a semi-precious gemstone. Some carnelians may have an orange-red hue.
Chalcedony	Chalcedony is micro-fibrous form of quartz.
Chert	A variety of fine-grained silica that contains micro crystals of quartz. It comes in form of a rock and is actually a nodule, which means it is a lump of mineral that has a contrasting composition to the sediment or sedimentary rock that encloses it. This happens during or after rock formation when a part of sedimentary rock changes into another sedimentary rock. When the nodule occurs in chalk, it is called Flint.
Faience	Faience is glazed earthenware coated with opaque colours. The Harappans used river clay to make potteries. These potteries were painted and then hardened by firing in special kilns (of which we shall see later). The end product was a coloured ceramic, which when fired by powdered quartz, gave a material known as faience. This material was then coated with copper and silica minerals to give it a shiny opaque glaze. Beads, bangles, figurines were the products that the artisans of that age produced.
Flaking	Flake in the context of making tools would be to take out a slice or a chip from a stone in order to make that tool or a blade.
Jasper	Jasper is a dense, opaque and impure variety of silica. It can be red, yellow, brown or green in colour. It is used as a gemstone.

Knapping	Knapping would be to give a final shape to a flake to make a tool. One could knap a chert or a flint flake to achieve that purpose.
Lapidary	Lapidary is an art of cutting, polishing or engraving precious stone. Lapidary is also referred to the artisan as also the art.
Lapis Lazuli	Lapis lazuli is a compact form of rock. It contains a mixture of minerals with lazurite as the main mineral. It has a deep blue colour and is classified as a semi-precious stone.
Microliths	A microlith is a small stone tool made of flint or chert. The smaller ones are about a centimetre in length and half a centimetre in width. These are attached to a spear or an arrow and used for hunting.
Steatite	Another name for soapstone, it being a variety of talc with a soapy feel. The Harappans used this material mostly to make seals.

The Harappan Civilisation 5

Most of us studied about what was called the Indus Valley Civilisation in school and did not read further on the subject unless we pursued a discipline in which this civilisation formed an integral part of the lesson. It would be a refresher for most of us if we were to go through the process of discovering this great civilisation, also called the Harappan Civilisation and the Indus-Sarasvati Civilisation. We would refer to it as the Harappan Civilisation in the following pages. This is based on the practice of naming a civilisation depending on which place it was unearthed first.

There were two river systems along which the major part of this civilisation grew. The rivers were the Indus and the Sarasvati. The Indus, also known as Sindhu, starts from the Tibetan plateau near lake Mansarovar, flows through Ladakh, Gilgit in Pakistan occupied Kashmir and Baltistan, turns southwest flowing through the entire length of Pakistan to merge into the Arabian sea near Karachi. Four of the five northern river systems namely the Jhelum, Chenab, Rabi and Beas merge into the Indus at various places in Pakistan.

The last of the five, the Sutlej joined the ancient Sarasvati. The Sarasvati was the eastern edge of the Indus Civilisation, which lay on the Indian side. It was only after the partition, when Indus sites were discovered on the Sarasvati plain, that the extent of the spread of the civilisation became known. The *Ṛigveda* mentions geographically the Sarasvati to be between the Yamuna in the east and the Sutlej on the west, before the latter joins the Sarasvati. The ancient Sarasvati, now identified with the Ghaggar, commenced its journey from the glaciers north of Garhwal, flowed through Panjab, Haryana and Rajasthan. In its travel through Pakistan, it came to be known as Hakra. Before going further south into the Rann of Kutch in the Arabian Sea, it is known by various names but its archaeological significance is diminished since no excavations were ever undertaken in that area.

Post partition, the Indus sites were also discovered in the area of Gujarat where Dholavira, Lothal and Surkotada showed ample evidence of the same flourishing civilisation.

As mentioned earlier, Harappa and Mohenjo-daro were excavated initially in 1921 and 1922 respectively. Mohenjo-daro was taken up for a full fledged excavation in 1931 by John Marshall and Harappa was taken up by Madho Swarup Vats in 1940. Since it was before partition and was confined to the Indus valley, it was given the name of Indus Valley Civilisation. After partition, these sites went over to Pakistan. Indian archaeologists, however, carried out excavations on the Indian side in Panjab, Haryana, Rajasthan and Gujarat. Today, there are more than hundred sites that are associated with the Harappan culture through all levels of Early, Mature and late Harappan stages of which larger ones have been excavated.

As you will see, the 'centre of gravity' of the Harappan Civilisation, in fact, lay in the Sarasvati valley.

This civilisation was a highly developed one, covering over one million square kilometres. Its western boundary was in Baluchistan in Pakistan and its easternmost, the upper Ganga-Yamuna Doab in Uttar Pradesh. This spanned 1600 kms. On the north, it stretched from Jammu and Kashmir to Daimabad in Maharashtra, some 1400 kms apart. Town-planning, agriculture, domestication of animals, sea-faring and trade with outside of the then India, a developed culture and tradition were its hallmark. In fact, this civilisation sustained on surplus of agricultural production and commerce. The society was organised in a hierarchy and the settlements suggest that people lived in accordance with it. There existed religion and rituals as indicated by seals discovered in the excavations. That there was a method of writing is also borne out by the seals. Trade via land and sea routes was prominent and the traded items included gold, silver, copper, lapis lazuli, shells to name a few.

The various stages of this civilisation are broken into periods. Period I refers to Early Harappan, Period II to Mature Harappan and Period III to Late or Post-Mature times. Important facets are as follows:

EARLY HARAPPAN PERIOD

The Early Harappan period is considered to be commencing from 3300 BCE till 2800-2600 BCE. This period marks the beginning of Bronze Age in India. It will be of interest to know that pre- 3300 BCE, the predecessors of Early Harappan period were connected to the Hakra culture, a name given to the culture by virtue of the Hakra river that flows on the erstwhile bed of river Sarasvati on the Pakistan side. There is evidence of Hakra culture in Kunal and Bhirrana, too. After Hakra culture, the early Harappan period takes over, the essential difference being that while the inhabitants of Hakra culture lived in pits and also moved about, the early Harappans were more fixed to a settlement that had walls and a roof. Early Harappan is further broken into Period IA and IB. Period IA did not have any fortification walls. Period IB had settlements that had fortification walls. The concept of Citadel, Lower town with houses generally along cardinal directions came into being in the Mature Harappan phase.

The excavations of Period I sites indicate agriculture, making of some kind of seals, beads, domestication of animals as being in existence at that time. Early Harappan graduated to Mature Harappan by 2600 BCE.

MATURE HARAPPAN PERIOD

The Mature phase of the Harappan Civilisation is datable from 2600 BCE till 1900 BCE. This period is considered to be the peak of this civilisation, with organised settlements, an established hierarchy and other features such as agriculture, granaries, warehouses, shipping, dockyards, trade, etc. Export and import will necessarily include weights, measures, inscribed seals, system of writing, all of which existed. As will be seen, land and sea routes had been established as early as 2600 BCE, a dating based on West Asian evidence. While the sea trades were destined to eastern part of Arabian Peninsula, Persian Gulf and Mesopotamia, the land routes were established to north-eastern Iran and Central Asia. This trade must have brought qualitative changes to the style of living in the form of larger settlements, bigger houses, assembly halls, etc. Fine jewellery suggests that ladies were inclined to dress themselves up.

Given the evidences obtained from the excavations, there were no palaces; however, there did exist a concept of 'Citadel' where lived the elites. What begs a question is how a region of over one million square kilometres could have such a remarkable standardisation. Some examples of standardisation across the length and breadth of thus civilisation include similar urban settlements, standard road-widths, similar weights, measures and seals, a standardised brick measurement (as we will see later), similar pottery, script, etc.

Obviously, there must have existed a hierarchy. Indus script could have given an insight, regrettably that hasn't been deciphered.

Metallurgy was a strong point of the Harappans. Gold, silver, copper, and bronze were in ample evidence.

Religion was practiced, starting from Early Harappan period. Discovery of Śiva *liṅgam* shows that the Hindu gods could be the object of prayers and sacrifices. There are enough seals that indicate that. A seal with a deity in the centre and cattle beside is indicative of Lord *Paśupati*. Religious rituals were prevalent and animal sacrificial pits have been discovered.

LATE HARAPPAN PERIOD

The Late Harappan period is considered from 1900 BCE till 1500 BCE. Most of the Harappan sites do not go into Late Harappan period.

The hypothesis that the decline of Indus Valley Civilisation was due to Aryan invasion was put forth by Sir Mortimer Wheeler. That myth is now busted and the fact that Aryan invasion never occurred is now well established. There was no immigration by outside people either, that caused the decline of the civilisation. Scholars like Dales, Lal and Shaffer believe that the decline was due to climate change that resulted in the drying up of Sarasvati river system. Kalibangan, Rakhigarhi, Banawali, to name a few, were abandoned in the Mature Period itself. Carbon-14 dating puts the last habitation of Kalibangan at 1900 BCE. The borings made in the bed of Ghaggar river adjacent to Kalibangan indicate that the drying up of Sarasvati was the cause of the abandonment of Kalibangan round 1900 BCE. In fact, the waters of the Sarasvati got diverted to the Yamuna due to tectonic upheaval, as shown by the findings of geologists on the subject. This made the habitants of Sarasvati basin move east to the upper Ganga basin. We will talk more about it in Section 2 when we see how the civilisation ended.

Major Harappan sites in India were Ropar in Panjab, Rakhigarhi and Banawali in Haryana, Kalibangan in Rajasthan and Dholavira, Surkotada and Lothal in Gujarat. We shall be going through some of the salient features when discussing some of the sites. We will see what the cities had to offer by way of our culture and its tradition. We would, of course, begin with Harappa and Mohenjo-daro since it was the discovery of these towns which told the world that we were 5000 years old. Other sites excavated in India will follow thereafter, highlighting the culture and the traditions that we inherited from this greatest civilisation of the world, ever.

6 The Evolution of the Harappan Civilisation along the Sarasvati River

The archaeological evidence that is available to us at present that can relate to the *first occupants* was found *in the Sarasvati valley* and goes back to fifth millennium BCE. These occupants can be called the forefathers of the Harappans since there does exist a cultural continuity from this period till the Mature and the Post-Mature Harappan stage. There is no evidence of *occupancy* before that, however, that is not to say that there were no people before that period. For instance, as the Sarasvati flows into Pakistan and is called *Hakra* there, microliths belonging to Neolithic age are found in Cholistan (on the Pakistan side which lies west of Suratgarh in Rajasthan); but since no excavations have been carried out, the evidence of occupation is not available.

Let us take a look at places, as we know of date, where the earliest occupations took place.

Bhirrana is in Fatehabad district of Haryana and lies between Hissar and Sirsa. The mound at village Bhirrana, 200mx150m, lies on the left bank of ancient Sarasvati, now called the Ghaggar. First excavations were carried out between 2003 and 2006 and then again in 2012. What was discovered gave us the first signs of occupancy. The people lived in pits dug into the ground. Many pits of various sizes were found (Fig. 6.1). The bigger ones were

Fig. 6.1. Bhirrana: Dwelling pits, Stage I. (Pl. 1)

about eight feet in diameter and about one and a half to two feet deep, adequate to accommodate two people. The walls of the pit and the floor were plastered with mud. The other pits contained charred remains of cattle heads, charred pottery and ash. There were pits that contained a U-shaped hearth evidently for cooking.

These people were in Copper age that was later than the Neolithic period. Arrowheads of copper testify to that. Crucibles containing copper indicated that some manufacturing process was in vogue. Also discovered were beads of agate, carnelian, jasper and lapis lazuli. These, along with chert blades, were a precursor to the Harappans.

The pottery found at Bhirrana is the same that was discovered in Cholistan and was called the 'Hakra ware'. Remember that it is the same river system, Sarasvati, giving adequate evidence of connection between the two places hundreds of miles apart. However, as mentioned earlier, Cholistan was explored but not

Fig. 6.2. Bhirrana: Mud Appliqué Ware. (Pl. 2)

excavated. Explorations, being surface level observations and findings, could give us a clue that the 'era' was the same as in Bhirrana and Kunal, discussed later.

The pots were made on wheel, a technique that is very much prevalent today. Globular in shape, they were decorated with a film of mud mixed with white calcareous granules that covered the entire pot. Designs were made on the mud film and these were then given the fire treatment to make it hard and longer lasting. While these were the 'Mud Appliqué Ware' (Fig. 6.2) there was another method of making designs called 'Incised Ware' on which these designs were made by incision before these were heated on fire (Fig. 6.3). The Harappans later made exquisite designs on their ceramic pots as the processes matured with age, continuing to use the wheel to make pots.

Carbon-14 method dates this period to fifth millennium BCE.

Kunal, also located in Haryana, in Hissar district, is not far from Bhirrana. Here, too, pit-dwellings were discovered. These

Fig. 6.3. Bhirrana: Deep Incised Ware. (Pl. 3)

were an improvement on Bhirrana. The base of the pit was hardened and there existed a provision to cover the pit from the sky overhead. Along the circumference of the pit, there were holes at regular intervals to indicate that poles could be pushed inside to make a roof for the pit.

The occupants were fully established in the copper age, using copper arrowheads and fish hooks for killing their small games.

Like at Bhirrana, cooking was done in separate pits. Potteries are similar: Mud Appliqué Ware and the Incised Ware. However, an improvement was a two-colour scheme: black and white!

Kunal also provides an insight into later years. Occupants improved upon earlier set-up. Some pits became larger than 3m in diameter and had a cooking hearth within the pit. Lesser of Mud Appliqué ware and more of black-and-white ware were discovered at levels that belonged to a later stage. Shapes of *peepal* leaves and peacock were found designed on the pots (Fig. 6.4).

The sizes of pots increased and the shapes showed improvement in form of jars and beakers. Terracotta cakes made their appearance.

As we will see later, *peepal*, peacocks and terracotta cakes continued into the Mature Harappan stage.

Let us call this the Stage I of evolution. It is prior to the Early Harappan Period. (Evolution will be discussed in terms of Stages).

Stage II of evolution is when the occupants felt the need to come out of pits and live on surface. Why?

The most compelling reasons are that digging is not required on a large scale, there is no restriction in area on the surface, and therefore there is availability of larger area to make a home with walls and roof on top to face the nature. This could only happen when the pit-dwellers evolved the technique of making bricks, giving rise to the concept of walls and roof, which in turn enhanced safety and security of the pit-dwellers.

Some semblance of order also came into being. Let us take the settings at Bhirrana first. Houses were constructed with mud bricks measuring 13x26x39 cm or 14x28x42 cm or 15x30x45 cm, all in a ratio of 1:2:3, the thickness, width and the length respectively. We will find a similar order in the Indus and Sarasvati valley later as the evolution progressed.

Antiquities also show a gradual advancement. Female figurines, chert blades, beads of semi-precious stones, bone points and terracotta bangles were discovered.

Pottery designs changed. Apart from *peepal* leaves and peacock, there were straight and wavy bands in bi-chrome; fish was added as were floral and faunal designs.

At Kunal too, occupants came out of pit-dwellings and constructed for themselves houses on the surface. These were made from mud bricks. The brick dimensions were same as at Bhirrana but in addition, a ratio of 1:2:4 was also discovered. The sizes were 9x18x36 cm and 11x22x44 cm. This particular ratio continued into Mature Harappan stage also. People became conscious of hygiene. Soakage jars were installed at homes. Grains were stored in small pits dug for the purpose with its walls coated

Fig. 6.4. Kunal: Painted pottery. (Pl. 4)

with a mixture of clay and lime, the latter being a good disinfectant.

From the excavations carried out at Kunal, it becomes evident that there had been a gradual improvement in lifestyles of Kunalians, as the experts put it, over three sub-stages, the observation being an outcome of excavating different levels of occupation. While there is no intention to go into the details of each sub-stage, it is interesting to know what have been the advancements.

Houses got bigger.

The Kunalians became more prosperous. Objects recovered from houses not only include large number of semi-precious stones but also include objects made of silver and gold apart from copper that we already know of. Incidentally, copper processing was localised in that a copper smelting furnace was discovered with crucibles containing molten metal sticking to it. Axes, arrowheads,

Fig. 6.5. Kunal: Spiralled bangles, silver. (Pl. 28)

fish hooks, inverted-V-shaped arrowheads and spearheads were all made from copper. One of the houses revealed plenty of gold and silver ornaments, wrapped in a silver sheet and buried into the ground. There were silver tiaras and silver armlet of spiralled bangles (Fig. 6.5), one that we will see on a 'dancing girl' discovered at Mohenjo-daro. Makes one wonder whether hiding the jar containing all of this and then burying it in a pit was 'hoarding', a possibility in that age!

In fact, many houses contained gold and silver ornaments. They were not hidden, though. There were beads of agate and lapis lazuli. The significance of discovering lapis lazuli lies in the fact that it is not a localised stone. The nearest that one would have it would have been Baluchistan or Afghanistan. Another such long-distance item found in this land-locked Kunal was shell. How did that happen? The presence of seals confirms trade with other regions. The seals are steatite and of shell and were a precursor to what we are going to find in Harappan stage. Some seals had perforation at the back. These were used for sealing commodities and hence the reference to trade activities.

One of the silver ornaments was a necklace with flat discular beads, perforated for it to be stringed. See Fig. 6.6 and you will notice that it bears a striking resemblance to one found of gold at Lothal (Fig. 6.7) belonging to Mature Harappan stage which was almost a thousand years later. Almost, because we don't have the dating for 'advanced' Kunal period.

Another site that came into being in Stage II is Rakhigarhi in Hissar district of Haryana. It is one of the largest sites of Harappan Civilisation. With an area of about 105 hectares, it boasts of

Pl. 1. Bhirrana: Dwelling pits, Stage I.

Pl. 2. Bhirrana: Mud Appliqué Ware.

Pl. 3. Bhirrana: Deep Incised Ware.

Pl. 4. Kunal: Painted pottery.

Pl. 5. Mohenjo-daro: Dancing Girl.

Pl. 6. Mohenjo-daro: Priest in limestone.

Pl. 7. Steatite seals from Dholavira.

Pl. 8. Lothal: Discular beads of gold with circular perforation.

Pl. 9. Mohenjo-daro: Gold disc beads.

Pl. 10. Mohenjo-daro: Gold necklace.

Pl. 11. Dholavira: Gold beads.

Pl. 13. Kalibangan: Bronze bull.

Pl. 12. Harappa: Killing of a buffalo to please deity.

Pl. 14. Banawali: Agate-bead necklace.

Pl. 15. Banawali: Pot with beads.

Pl. 16. Dholavira: Rock-cut reservoir.

Pl. 17. Nausharo: Use of vermilion.

Pl. 18. Nausharo: Use of vermilion.

Pl. 19. Mohenjo-daro: Swastika motif engraved on a seal.

Pl. 20. Entrance to a Hindu house with Swastika symbol.

Pl. 21. Harappa: A terracotta figurine greeting with 'namaste'.

Pl. 23. Gold cone from Mohenjo-daro.

Pl. 22. Lady wearing spiralled bangles.

Pl. 24. Conical ornament and bangles.

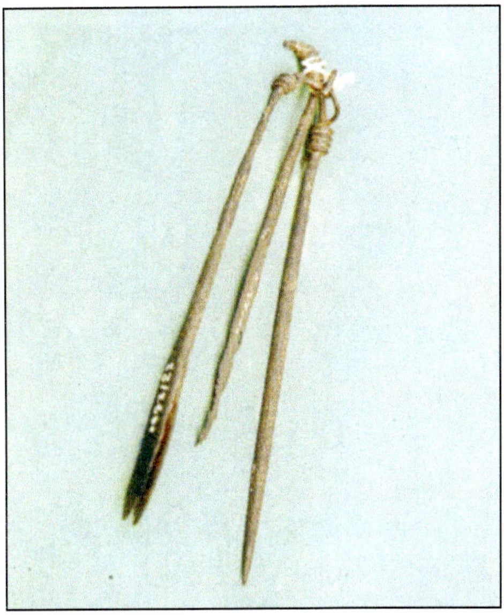

Pl. 25. A three-in-one toiletry item in copper from Harappa.

Pl. 26. A modern three-in-one toiletry item, copper.

Pl. 27. A stage in bead-making process.

Pl. 28. Kunal: Spiralled bangles, silver.

Pl. 29. Gold disc-beads from Lothal.

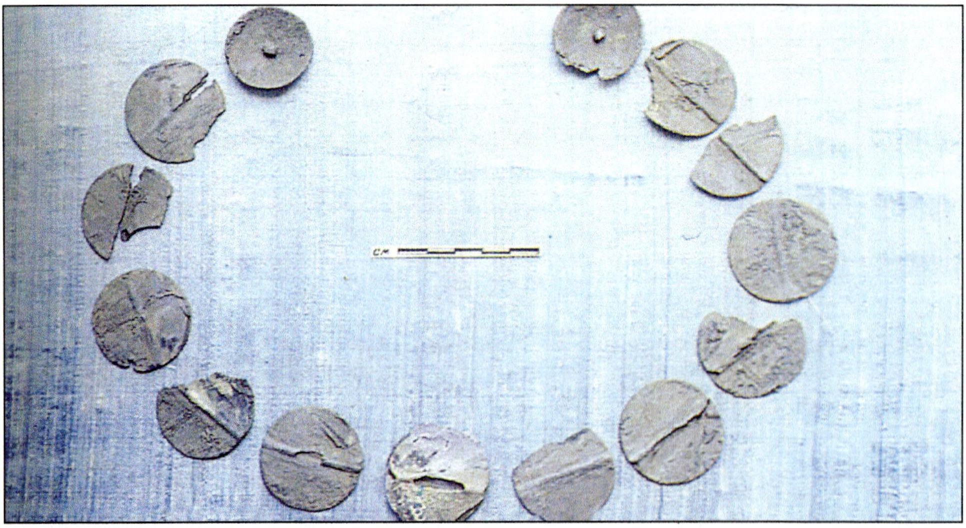

Pl. 30. Silver discular beads from Kunal for a necklace.

Pl. 31. Śiva *liṅga*-cum-*yoni* in a modern temple.

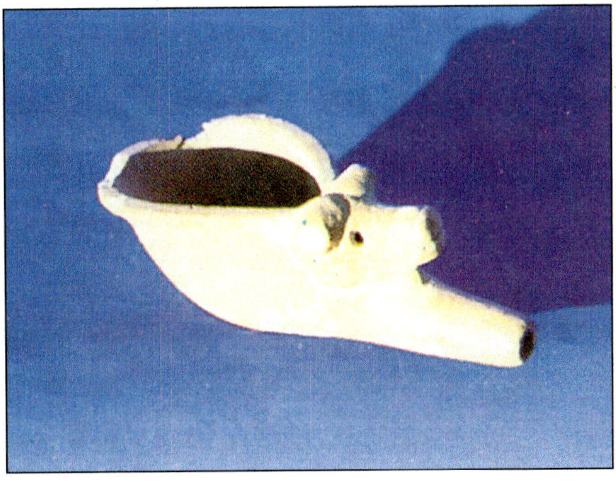

Pl. 32. A terracotta feeding cup from Kalibangan.

Pl. 33. A terracotta cage with birds, from Harappa.

Pl. 34. A modern cage.

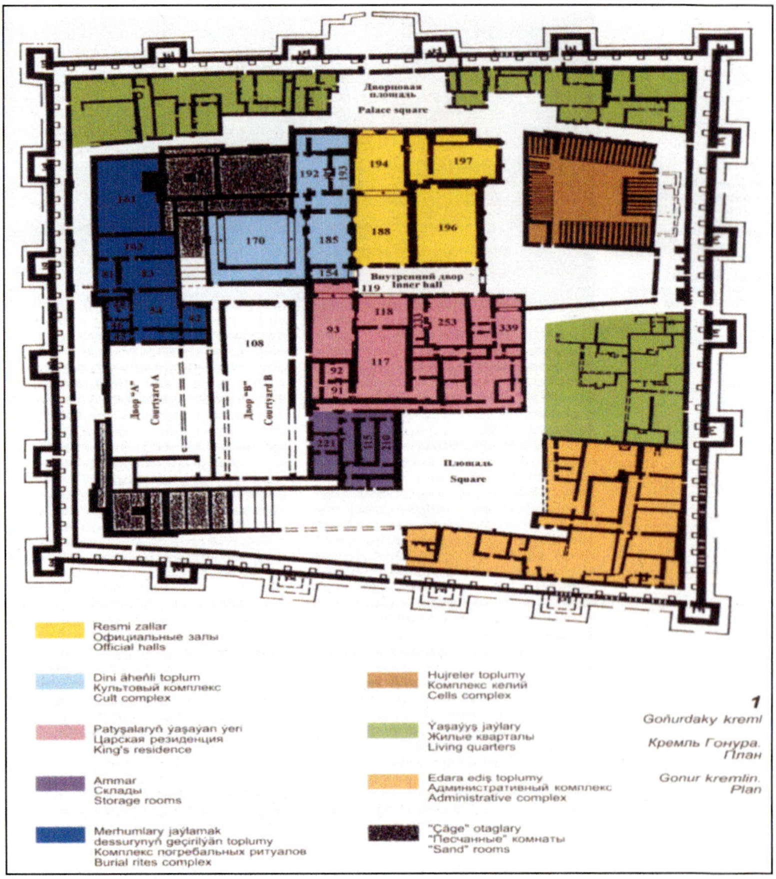

Pl. 35. Gonur, Margiana: Plan of Citadel.

Pl. 36. Bactria: Silver ceremonial axe.

Pl. 37. Bactria: Composite stone figure.

Pl. 38. Feline in semi-precious stone inlay.

Pl. 39. Migration of people as mentioned in *Baudhayāna Śrautasūtra*.

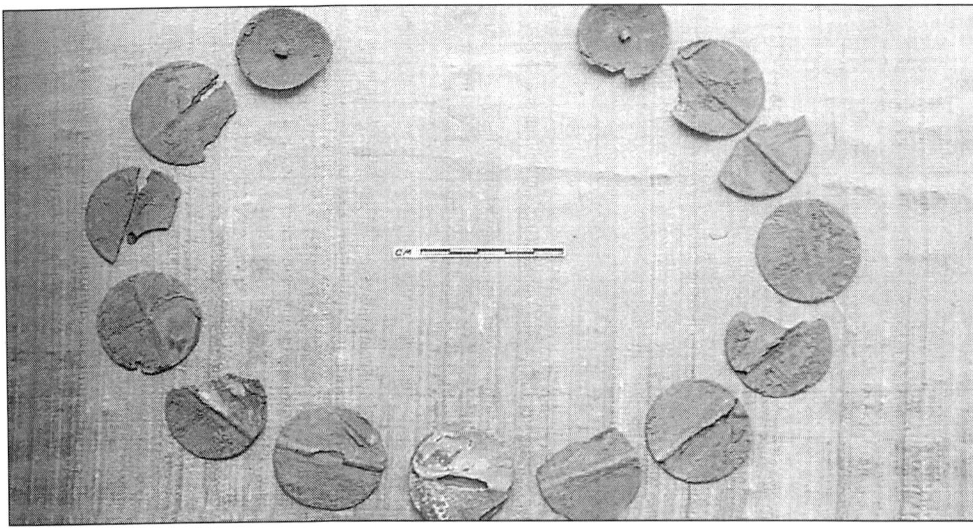

Fig. 6.6. Kunal: Discular beads of silver with axial perforations. (Pl. 30)

continuity from Pre-Harappan up to Mature Harappan, going past Stage III into Stage IV, definitions of which we will discuss a little later. That this is so is evident by the site having four structural periods. The excavator divided the area into seven parts for the ease of reporting findings and specifying periods.

Though the population data collected is sparse, certain things do stand out for the purpose of knowing about how the evolution was progressing. The houses are larger with rooms around a central courtyard, a feature that became common in the Mature Harappan period. They were along cardinal directions and the bricks used to construct the houses were in the ratio of 1:2:3. Construction of houses was with mud bricks. In one of the parts excavated, the lanes measured 1.6 m. Through the lane flowed a drain, constructed with kiln-fired bricks. The kiln, therefore, now comes into being due to realisation of the fact that the bricks would be sturdier, longer lasting and, most importantly, capable of withstanding water flow.

Amongst the artefacts discovered were pots akin to 'Mud Appliqué Ware' and 'Incised Ware' as at Bhirrana and Kunal. Also, there were bi-chrome wares and, in addition, some grey wares.

Also found were arrowheads, copper bangles, steatite beads, terracotta figurines and cart models. The cart models do signify transfer of heavy loads across the land. Do remember the steatite seals with perforations that were attached to the commodities.

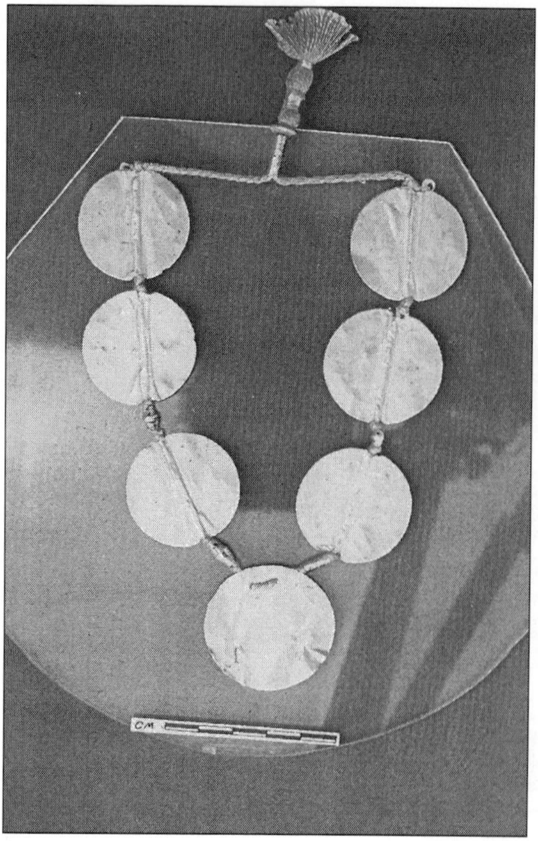

Fig. 6.7. Lothal: Discular beads of gold with axial perforations. (Pl. 8)

Stage III, also known as the Early Harappan Period, can be described as a period when the concept of peripheral fortification walls came into being. Remember that the colonies were getting larger and population increasing. Was security the main concern? Not as far as we can see from the knowledge gained from post-Harappan era. Evidence is clear that from stage I to beyond the Mature Harappan period (Ok, so this is Stage IV) into the post-Harappan, we find that there was no attack either from the invaders from outside the civilisation or was there an intra-civilisation conflict. It is not clear as to what was the reason for fortification of cities in Stage III.

Kalibangan was a classic example of this stage. It lay on the banks of ancient Sarasvati, now the dried Ghaggar in the Hanumangarh district of Rajasthan. It progressed from Stage III to Stage IV with a break of about a century, having been abandoned at Stage III due to an earthquake (Fig. 6.8). The fortification commenced during Stage III, around 3100 BCE. The entire town was fortified.

The pottery at Kalibangan that belongs to Stage III is a 'carry forward' of the previous stages. It has both, the Hakra Appliqué

Ware as well as the Incised Ware. The quantity of bi-chrome pottery is much less. It also has shapes and designs that became the hallmark of Stage IV. Notable amongst these are the tall cylindrical vases, large jars, dishes- and cups-on-stand and others. The fine grained, red fired ware with black painted designs come into being and which is found in abundance in the next stage.

Tools discovered are microliths which are, reminiscent of Hakra tools of Stage I; and there also exist long fine blades of chert, a feature of Stage IV.

We will go through the finds of Kalibangan in a later chapter as also of Banawali, a site that stretched from Stage II till Stage IV.

Fig. 6.8. Kalibangan: Faulted strata resulting from an earthquake.

Stage IV of this civilisation is the 'Mature Harappan Period'. It commences from about 2600 BCE and continues till about 1900 BCE. Its main characteristic is that the there is a segregation of society into a so called 'higher class' and the 'rest'. It is in this stage that the concept of 'Citadel' and 'Middle and /or Lower Town' came into being. There was an emergence of a system of writing, of weights and measures and seals and sealings, the last one as a regular feature of trade unlike irregular and scant occurrences of previous stages.

We will be discussing the salient features and famous towns of Stage III and IV in subsequent chapters.

7 Salient Features of the Harappan Civilisation

Before we take up the findings at some major Harappans sites in India and Pakistan, it would be good to have a look at the salient features of this civilisation.

TOWN PLANNING

The most important feature in the Mature Harappan stage of this civilisation was its town planning. It represented an advanced and a well established urban civilisation. There existed a Citadel, Middle Town and a Lower town in most of the Mature Harappan sites excavated.

A Citadel could be defined as an area, either fortified by walls or not, that may have housed the higher hierarchy and which could have included priests. It housed 'one of its type' facility of the township. For example, excavations have unearthed structures like 'The Great Bath', 'Granary' or the 'Assembly Hall'. While these were located in the Citadel area, it cannot be established that these may have been meant for use of all members of the community.

In a township, there could be a Middle town and the Lower town. Or there could be only one of them. If there existed only one of them, it housed the middle class gentry as well as the lower class. If there existed both of them then the lower town would house the artisans, the workmen and other lower functionaries.

Fig. 7.1. Dholavira: Covered drain with inspection holes.

Harappan settlements were generally planned on a grid pattern. The streets were oriented along north-south and east-west. The widths of the streets were in a fixed ratio. If the smallest of them was one unit wide, the next higher was two units and the third, three units. This planning was not a feature of West Asian sites of that age. However, in the context of Harappan Civilisation, this was true of urban settlement; the rural settlement, of whatever is known, did not conform to this.

The construction of houses was of mud bricks, or kiln-fired bricks. The size of bricks was in the ratio of 4:2:1, being its length, breadth and thickness. The houses used bricks measuring 30x15x7.5 cms and fortification walls, 40x20x10 cms. In Kutch, stones were used for construction since these were available in plenty.

A typical middle class house consisted of a courtyard with rooms around its three sides. On the fourth side there was an entrance, wide enough for a bullock cart to come in. This entrance was on the street side. Courtyard provided for water and fodder for the cattle and for cooking for the household. Quite a few houses had their private wells. Some of the larger houses had staircases, indicating the possibility of a floor above.

Apart from houses, there were large buildings for common use. In Mohenjo-daro, for example, there was an Assembly Hall, a Granary and what has been termed as a Great Bath. Harappa, too, had a granary. Lothal had a large dockyard, the most unique feature of contemporary civilisation anywhere in the world. Alongside the dockyard was a warehouse that complemented the dockyard.

At Kalibangan it was noted that on the outside of the entrance, on its either side, there were platforms for the people to sit on. While excavating at this site in 1960s, the excavator noted that almost every house in the nearby villages had similar platforms built on either side of entrance of the houses.

Sanitation and hygiene were accorded high priority. There was usually a room for bath from where the water drained out to a jar placed immediately outside the house in the street. The streets had sometimes a covered drainage system. Mohenjo-daro, for example, had an elaborate underground system of drainage. There were cesspits at intervals so that sullage could be removed at regular intervals (Fig. 7.1).

AGRICULTURE

The second most important feature of the civilisation was its agriculture. It was on this that the economy seems to have been built. Wheat and barley were the main crops. Cotton was also produced, and that was not so in either West Asia or Egypt in the third millennium BCE. In fact, Mehrgarh, a site going back to fifth millennium BCE, has shown evidence of cotton. Cloth was used for packaging of export bundles.

Rice was not found in the Indus valley during the mature Harappan stage. However, rice-husk has been found at Lothal in Gujarat. In the late Harappan stage, rice has been reported from sites in the upper Ganga-Yamuna doab. Millets of at least six varieties were reported. Mustard and horse grams were grown in Rajasthan, Panjab, Haryana and western UP.

Terracotta representations of plough, discovered at Mohenjo-daro and at Banawali, indicate that the fields were ploughed before being sown. The earliest agriculture field discovered at Kalibangan in Rajasthan, which dates back to Early Harappan period, has shown ploughed fields in which cross furrows indicate the use of

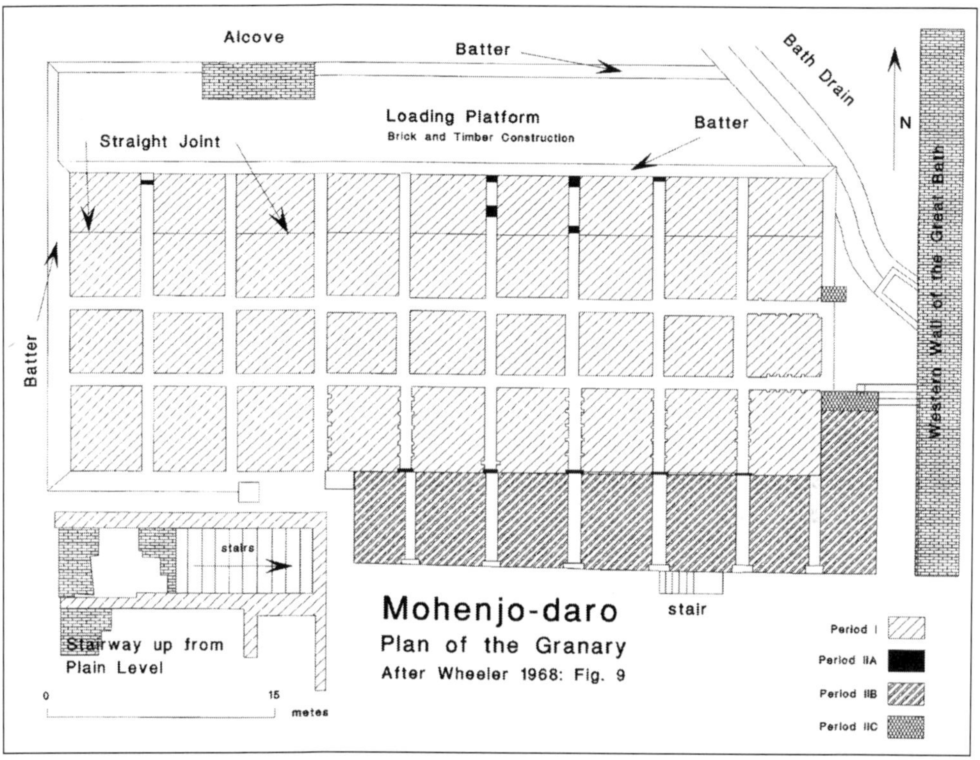

Fig. 7.2. Mohenjo-daro: Plan of Granary.

plough. It also indicates that two crops were grown in one field, but more on this later. Copper/bronze sickles as well as chert blades with sharp cutting edges were used for harvesting.

Large-sized granaries indicate that the produce was in big quantities. Production was in abundance. A plan of granary at Mohenjo-daro is at Fig. 7.2. The granary was 45 x 22.5 m and had twenty-seven square and rectangular blocks, arranged in three rows of nine each. These lay east-west. Each block was separated from the other by a passage. Most likely, on these blocks there stood a superstructure of wood. Another granary was excavated at Harappa, which we shall see later.

Storage facilities were also found in houses. In Kalibangan, seven storage jars were found in a house. Elsewhere, too, storage facilities have been seen.

The principal cereals have been wheat and barley. There were three varieties of wheat that were cultivated. Similarly, barley had three varieties. Rice was not known in Indus or the Sarasvati valley but in Gujarat, rice husks have been found. Six varieties of millets have been discovered. Of these, only one type is found in Lothal and others in Rojdi, also in Gujarat area. Sesame and mustard were used for cooking and for lighting lamps. An interesting discovery is of cotton. It did not exist in Egypt, for which it had become famous, in the third millennium BCE, whereas it was grown in India. Ample evidence of it has been found in sealing of parcels and packages. In fact, the cultivation of cotton in South Asia goes back to fifth millennium BCE, evidence of which is found in Mehrgarh, although the site was not a part of Indus valley.

Henna and ornamental flowers have been identified. Grapevine cultivation was very much in vogue. All these were identified by testing out corresponding charcoal remains by the Birbal Sahni Institute of Botany, Lucknow.

ANIMAL HUSBANDRY

Evidence of domestication of animals is available to us from Harappan seals, faunal remains and terracotta figures. As mentioned elsewhere the most famous domesticated animal has been humped bull, also called the 'zebu'. As a 'beast of burden', it was used for ploughing fields, transporting goods by pulling carts and even on its back. Cow, of course, was present for supplying all the milk and products thereof. Sheep and goat were domesticated for food. So were pigs and fowls. Their charred bones bear testimony to that.

Fish and turtles were also used for food. Of the many fish varieties found, *khaki, singhari* and *rohu* were prominent. The occurrence of large number of copper fishing hooks all over the Harappan sites confirms that angling was a serious business for procuring food.

Wild animals were hunted for food, too. Faunal remains of *nilgai* (a large Indian antelope), *sambhar* (a variety of Indian deer), *barasingha* (a swamp deer), spotted deer and blackbuck confirm this.

Buffalo was domesticated as was the elephant. Apart from using elephants for carriage of loads, it provided the ivory that was the hallmark of Harappan craftsmanship in women's decorative wear and toiletries.

Camels and horses are not to be found on seals. However, remains of camels were discovered at Mohenjo-daro, Kalibangan, Harappa and Surkotada, a site in the Kutch region of Gujarat.

Horse remains have been reported from Kalibangan, Lothal and Surkotada. A lot of debate whether horse was present during the Harappan times did take place but the subsequent study has confirmed its presence in the Harappan period.

Cats and dogs were kept as pets. There is a terracotta figure of a collared dog! Did we copy that from those times? Parrots, too, were kept as pets.

TRANSPORT

Transport is a necessary adjunct to trade. Evidence shows that cattle, and maybe, sheep and goat were used for surface transport. Carts for transportation of goods have been found to be five

Fig. 7.3. Nausharo: Terracotta model of cart.

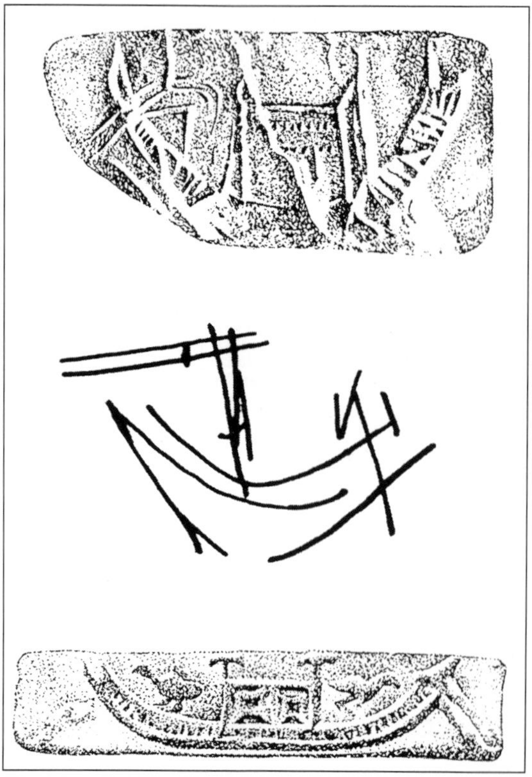
Fig. 7.4. Engraving of a boat on a tablet.

different types. Perhaps, each region designed one for its use. Fig. 7.3 shows a terracotta model of a cart from Nausharo. Bronze model has been found at Harappa. It is interesting to note that the distance between the corresponding pairs of ruts of wheels as discovered at Harappa was the same as now in Sindh.

Boats have been used for riverine transportation. Fig. 7.4 shows a tablet that has an engraving of a boat. Excavations at Lothal have featured five terracotta boat models. Coloured boats have been depicted on pots at Lothal.

Sea-faring boats would have required sails and oars. The travel to Mesopotamia via the Gulf route would have definitely depended upon the monsoon winds. That would have also been true of the return trip.

USE OF METALS

Metals were used variously for domestic and agricultural purposes. These were also used for making weapons, and on the other end of spectrum, for objet d'art!

Use of copper and bronze, an alloy of copper and tin, was predominant. Copper was also alloyed with arsenic, lead and nickel but tin was most common. Other metals included lead, silver and gold.

Tools of copper and bronze included flat axes and axes with a shaft hole, chisels, straight and curved saws, nails, chains, drills,

Fig. 7.5. Dholavira: Arrowhead and chisels.

sickles for harvesting, longer chisels probably for attaching to a plough, all to meet the ends of domestic and agricultural purposes.

Weapons included arrows and spearheads. These were perhaps for killing animals for food, since in the entire civilisation, there appears to be no evidence of warfare. If there was, then perhaps some body-armour, helmets and shields too would have been discovered.

Pots and pans too were made of copper and bronze. These were same as their earthen counterparts. *Handis*, long-handled frying pans, vases and goblets are amongst those discovered.

Articles that were made of metal for daily use of women were bangles, rings and hairpins. Varieties of ear-studs were also found.

Fig. 7.6. Nausharo: Copper spearhead and arrowhead.

Fig. 7.7. Mohenjo-daro: Dancing Girl. (Pl. 5)

Use of silver was common for making ornaments, though there are silver vessels too. There are findings of gold ornaments. Beads were common to silver and gold. Gold dominated necklaces, pendants, rings and amulets.

Of lead, not many objects have been found. However, these included vases and plumb bobs.

Metal art included figures of humans and animals. Dancing girl (Fig. 7.7) discovered from Mohenjo-daro is a classic example.

Animal figurines included bull, buffalo, dog, elephant and a few others.

USE OF STONE

Stone technology is as old as the Palaeolithic times. Long and short blades were crafted for various purposes including hunting.

In the context of Harappan Civilisation, stone was also used for producing art objects in Harappa and Mohenjo-daro. It was used in architecture in Dholavira and a few other sites in Kutch where it was readily available. Large stones were carved to make pillars at Dholavira for the buildings. See Fig. 7.8. Don't they denote near-perfection?

Fig. 7.8. Dholavira: Stone pillars.

Fig. 7.9. Mohenjo-daro: Priest in limestone. (Pl. 6)

Human figures, most famous being that of a priest in limestone (Fig. 7.9), are some of the examples of stone sculptures. It is 18 cms in height with lower part not found. One can see the meditative and a peaceful face. He wears a well groomed beard, and a shawl that passes under the right arm and goes over the left shoulder covering his left arm. Isn't that the way we still see some *sādhūs* wearing a shawl!

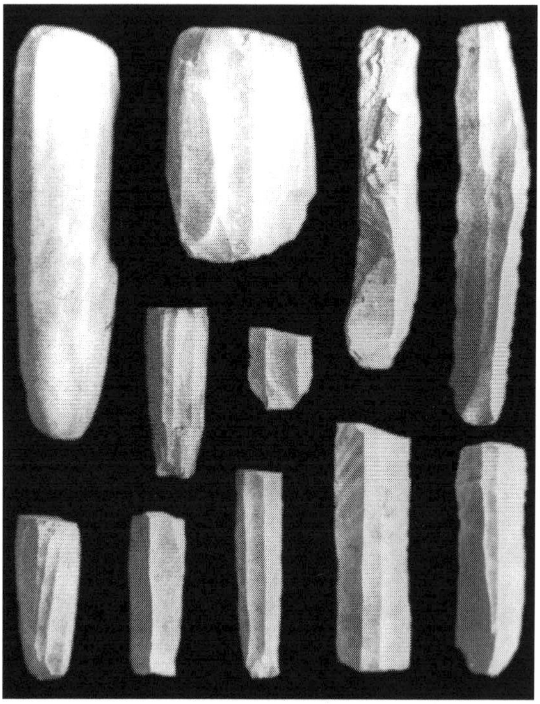

Fig. 7.10. Harappan chert blades.

Stone statuettes found at Harappa and Mohenjo-daro are the only finds of stone sculptures; there are no finds in the Sarasvati valley.

Stone was also used for making tools that could be used for agriculture and for felling trees. It appears that chert (chert being fine-grained sedimentary rock) and limestone were used for the purpose. Such tools were found across the civilisation indicating that they were manufactured at a major hub and distributed to other centres. See Fig. 7.10.

Interesting also is the use of chert for making weights, which were cubical in shape. More on weights later.

USE OF CLAY

Clay was readily available since the civilisation was spread along the river systems. Its foremost use was for making pots and pans. And the next easy thing was to make terracotta figurines. It was yet another medium to express art and craft, apart from metal and stone. The figures were made by hand and a majority of them are animal figures. All animals that are found on seals have been made in clay too. Examples are bulls, rhinoceros and

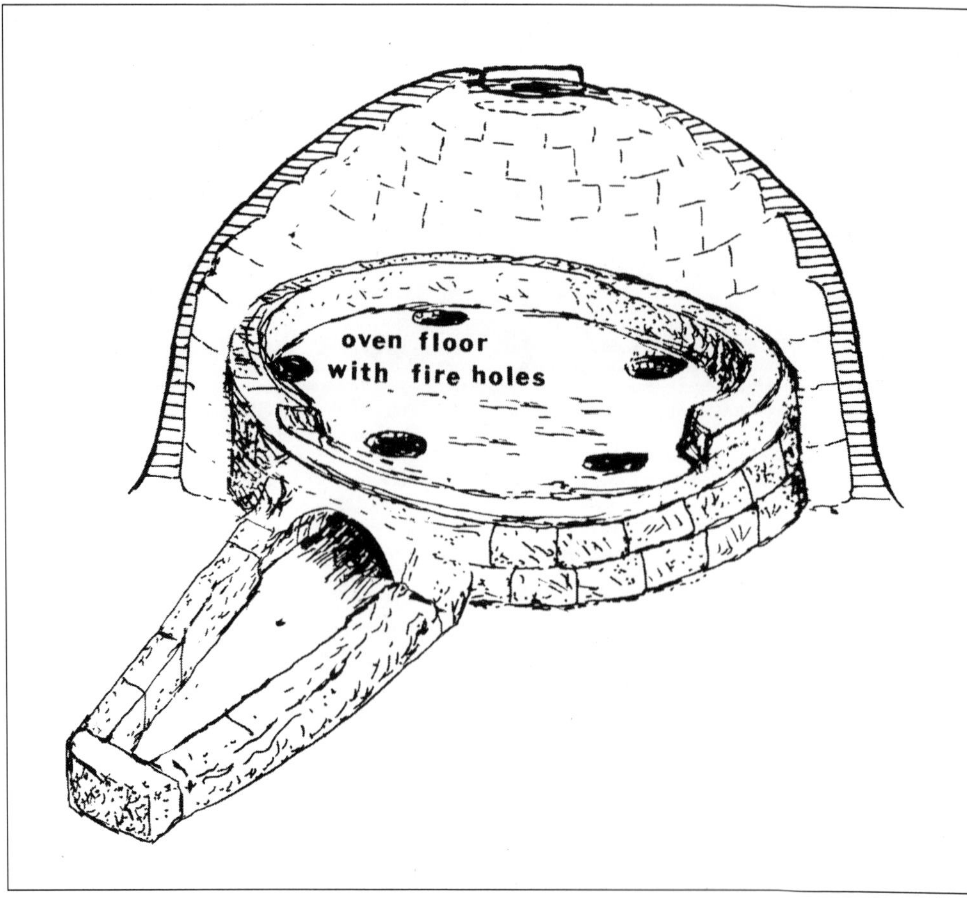

Fig. 7.11. Kiln model.

elephants. Next to animals, human figures were common, the majority being the female figures. Then there is a set of figures that represents the yogic *āsanas.*

Clay potteries were made by hand if they were flattish, else on potter's wheel. The pottery included *hāṇḍīs* for cooking and vessels for storing food. Plates and drinking tumblers were also made of clay. There were storage jars, medium and large-sized, both. These were kiln-fired. The pots were usually painted with floral and geometric motifs but sometimes with human figures too. The designs were in black. But more on potteries follows.

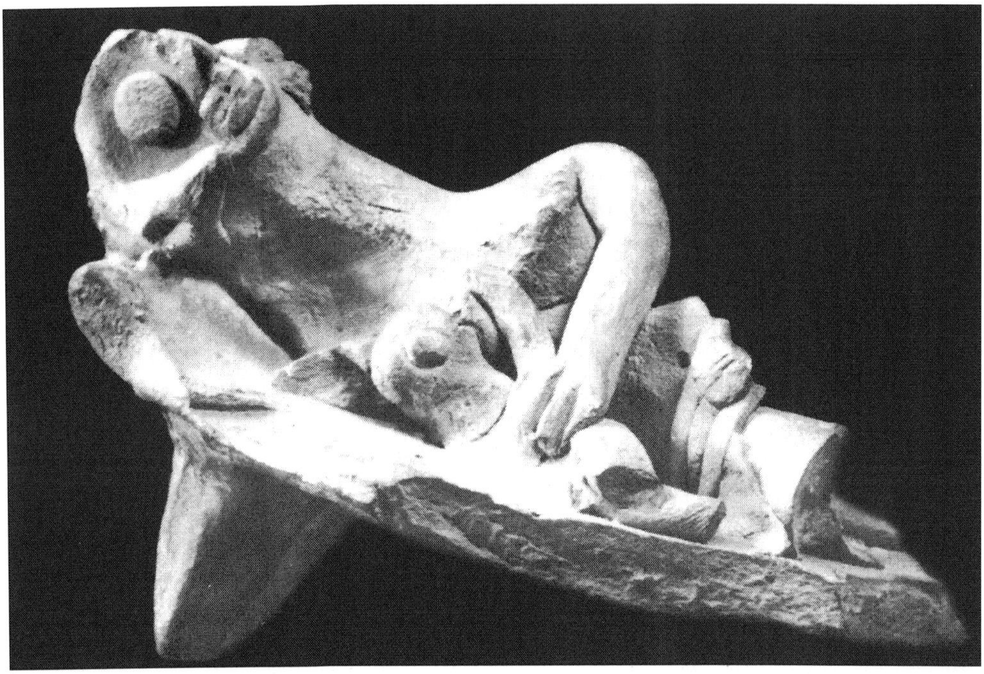

Fig. 7.12. Female, breast-feeding a child.

A word about the kiln. The kiln had two chambers, one above the other and separated by a horizontal partition that had evenly spaced holes (Fig. 7.11). The lower chamber had an opening which allowed firewood to be pushed inside. The fire thus heated up the upper chamber on which clay pots were placed. No change over these many years!

Terracotta artefacts are aplenty. These mainly depicted human figures, both male and female, animals and other objects. Fig. 7.12 shows a mother breast-feeding her child. Another shows birds in a cage (Fig. 7.13).

Fig. 7.13. Birds in a cage.

POTTERIES

Harappan potteries were made of well levigated clay, i.e. clay smoothened out by thorough grinding and kneading. These were wheel-turned, well fired in the kiln that resulted in sturdy red ware. These were often slipped, that is, given a coating and designs made on them. The designs were largely floral and straight line drawings. A few of them had human and animal forms. A sample of potteries is at Fig. 7.14

How to read the pottery? Well, seen from the front, the drawing is divided into two halves that are split vertically. The right half is how one sees the pottery from outside. Left half is the section drawing. To make the understanding of section drawing clearer, imagine viewing the pottery from the top. Divide it into four quarters. Number them as: front left as 1, left back as 2, right back as 3 and right front as 4. The left half of the drawings shown in the figure is quarter no 2 as viewed from front. The darker line on the left half shows the thickness of the pot. Comparing it with the scale that is in centimetres, ring stand (item 1) was about one centimetre in thickness and the basin in the lower row, about 2.5 centimetres thick.

The pot forms above were necessitated by daily requirements. There were *hāṇḍīs* for cooking, there were large but shallow bowls for cooked food. These were covered with lids, some of which often had knobs. *Chaklās* were used to prepare *rotīs*, or its equivalent. Platters have been found which must have been used as plates for eating. For drinking water, there were beakers and cups. Pointed bottom goblets may have served the same purpose, and since they could not have rested on their bottoms, they must have been put upside down after use.

Storage pottery for water and grains were large jars. Some of these had narrow bottom, to be embedded into the ground (?). Some jars were painted. (See Fig. 7.15). They could also have been placed on ring stands.

The use of stands for dishes and cups was a normal feature. Dishes could have been for solids and cups for liquids. The large basins were for washing, perhaps dishes or even clothes. The bowl

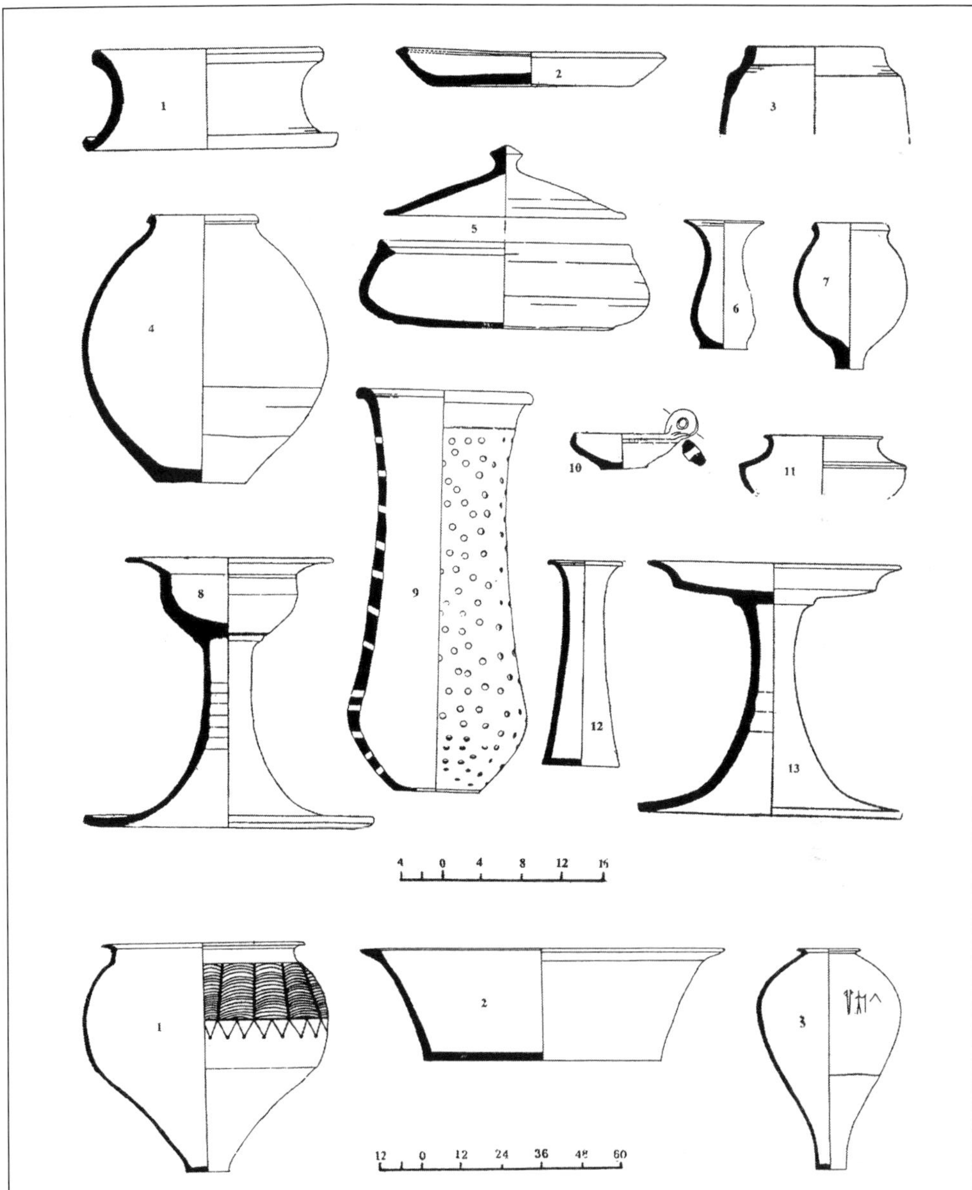

Item: 1. Ring stand, 2. Dish, 3. Jar, 4. Jar, 5. Casket with lid, 6. Beaker, 7. Goblet, 8. Cup-on-stand, 9. Perforated jar, 10. Bowl or cup with pinched up lips, 11. Pot, 12. Beaker, 13. Dish on stand.
Bottom Row (note the change in scale): 1. Jar, 2. Basin, 3. Pointed bottom goblet with inscription.

Fig. 7.14. Pottery types, Harappan Civilisation.

Fig. 7.15. Lothal: Painted jar.

Fig. 7.16. Harappa: Some painted designs on pottery.

or cup with pinched up lips could have been used for providing light, the pinched up being used for holding the wick. The conclusion is based on soot marks that were present on such a bowl.

The tall cylindrical jar with perforations (item 9, Fig. 7.14) gave rise to many imaginations, a few of them being a container for burning coal to keep warm, for extraction of juice of Soma plant to make *soma-rasa* as cited in the Vedic verses. But it could also have been used for keeping vegetables or other foodstuff which do require ventilation, if kept for long periods.

The painted designs contained all aspects of Harappan life. Starting from simple straight lines designs, the designs went on to display complex drawings that contained humans, flora and fauna. Floral motifs included rosettes, *peepal* leaf, banana and acacia. Faunal drawings contained peacock, crane, goats, and others. See Fig. 7.16

SEALS

Seals found at the Harappan sites greatly add to our knowledge of the way of life of the people. Engravings on these seals reveal a very high level of craftsmanship. Classic examples often quoted are those of the *Brahmani* bull and unicorn, both from Mohenjo-daro. Seals of unicorn, a mythical horse with one spiralled horn, are maximum in numbers. More than half of the seals discovered at Mohenjo-daro are of unicorn whereas at Harappa, these are slightly less than half of the seals discovered. (See Figs. 7.17-7.19.)

Seals were made from steatite, which is another name for soapstone. Soapstone is soft and easy to engrave. Once engraved, the seals were heated up to make them hard.

Over two thousand seals have been found and these were discovered in almost every major urban centre of the civilisation. With every new excavation, the numbers continue to add up. The seals varied in size and shape but were mostly squarish, two to seven cms on each side. Some seals, however, were rectangular or circular.

Fig. 7.17. Steatite seals from Dholavira. (Pl. 7)

Fig. 7.18. Mohenjo-daro: Seal depicting a bull.

Fig. 7.19. Mohenjo-daro: Seal depicting a unicorn.

Use of seals appears to be twofold. One was to indicate ownership. Most of the seals have human figures, deities, scripts and animals. The most common seals were of animals with a script written on them. Animals included tiger, rhinoceros, water buffalo, goat, crocodiles, elephant and bulls. It is very much possible that these indicated the ownership of a group, place or particular strata of society. These were also inscribed with a symbol or some text on top.

Seals were also used for commercial purposes, mainly for markings on trade parcels. A lump of clay was put on what bound the parcel and the owner's seal was stamped on it, just like the way it is done today on official mails where a string joint is stamped. This can be inferred from clay sealings that bear impressions of string or cord. There could be one or more seals on the parcel. Also, elephant seals are found in large quantities in Harappa and Mohenjo-daro and also in Kalibangan and Lothal indicating that there existed internal trade between the large and small cities. In a warehouse at Lothal, which had caught fire, as many as sixty-five sealings were discovered. These had been affixed to the packages that had been temporarily stored there for export.

IVORY, SHELLS AND BEADS

Items of ivory were not common across the civilisation but were limited to Mohenjo-daro and Lothal. Most of the items depict that ivory was used for ladies' toiletries. At Lothal, a small tapered ivory rod with paint mark was discovered. Can it be a third millennium BCE lipstick? Other ivory items were comb, hair pins, handle for combs and ear-studs.

Shells were aplenty around the coastal areas. Area around the Gulf of Kutch right up to the coastal areas west of Karachi could have given enough shells to meet the requirements of ladies. While the *shankh* was the obvious first product, finished items from shells included beads, bangles, pendants, rings and bracelets. Other items included knives, engravers and gamesmen. Shell, both as a raw

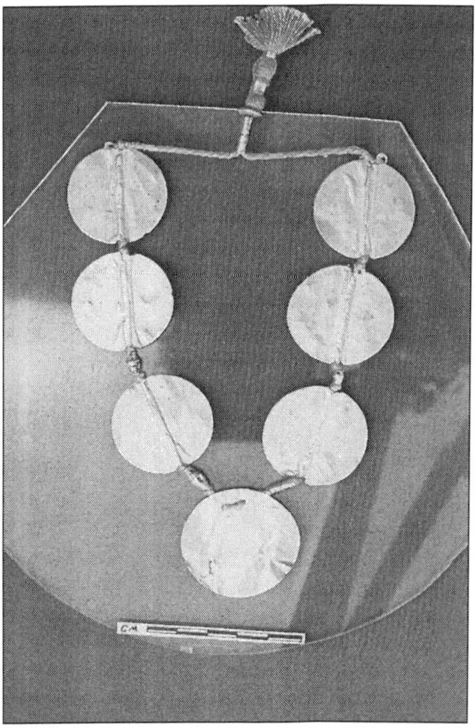

Fig. 7.20. Lothal: Discular beads of gold with circular perforation. (Pl. 8)

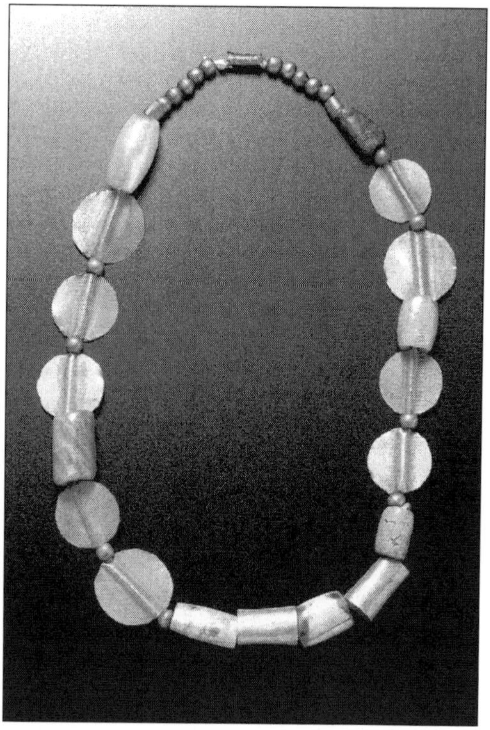

Fig. 7.21. Mohenjo-daro: Gold disc beads. (Pl. 9)

Fig. 7.22. Mohenjo-daro: Gold necklace. (Pl. 10)

material, and its product in final form were traded between large and smaller cities.

Bead-making dates back to a couple of millennia before the Mature Harappan period. Even before the bead-making expertise grew to the highest levels, simple methods were adopted to make ornaments. Using softer raw materials and simple stone tools of the period, the end product was indeed more than presentable. As the civilisation matured, so did the processes. The requirements of trade, of the elites as also the commoners necessitated a marked increase in production requirements. Numbers of production workshops increased as did the range of raw materials. Softer raw materials were no longer an issue; stones were shaped to make beads as were the hard gemstones like carnelian and jasper. Naturally, the drills and cutting tools became specialised.

The use of heat on certain raw materials gave a whole new dimension to the look of the stone. The new look could give a change of colour, change of hardness and also the reflectivity quotient. The lapidaries exploited the fire treatment to make the beads an item that was perhaps the best amongst all the contemporary civilisations of the world.

So we see the beads as the most popular form to go into the making of an ornament in the Mature Indus period. Made from gold, silver, copper, shells, agate, carnelian, lapis lazuli and a few semi-precious stones, the bead-based ornaments were discovered across the civilisation. Gujarat was the hub for manufacture of beads. A full-fledged bead factory was discovered in Lothal by its excavator. In a large courtyard there was a working platform. The courtyard was surrounded by eleven rooms. Two earthen jars were found embedded in the platform, one containing 582 beads of carnelian and the other containing 212 beads of carnelian, shell and steatite. There were beads with white-on-red designs and with black-on-white designs. The carnelian beads were exported and have been found at many sites in West Asia.

Fig. 7.23. Dholavira: Gold beads. (Pl. 11)

It may be of interest to know that Gujarat is still the hub of bead-making industry in India.

Semi-precious stones that were used for making beads also included agate, onyx, jasper, chalcedony, crystal, amethyst, lapis lazuli and turquoise, the last two being imports from Afghanistan and Turkmenistan respectively. Harappans had the wherewithal to fuse lime with quartz at extremely high temperature to make faience beads!

TRADE

There is a consensus amongst scholars that a civilisation can grow to such a scale as did the Indus Valley if two criteria are met. These are production of food on a large scale so as to sustain population and secondly, if there exists a riverine system to support irrigation for continued agriculture and also a transportation system capable of operating on a river. Evidently, the river Indus and the Sarasvati, along with their tributaries, met the required criterion for internal trade.

Apart from the river route, there was, of course, the land route. And towards the Mature Harappan stage, in the second half of the third millennium BCE, the sea route to the Gulf areas was also

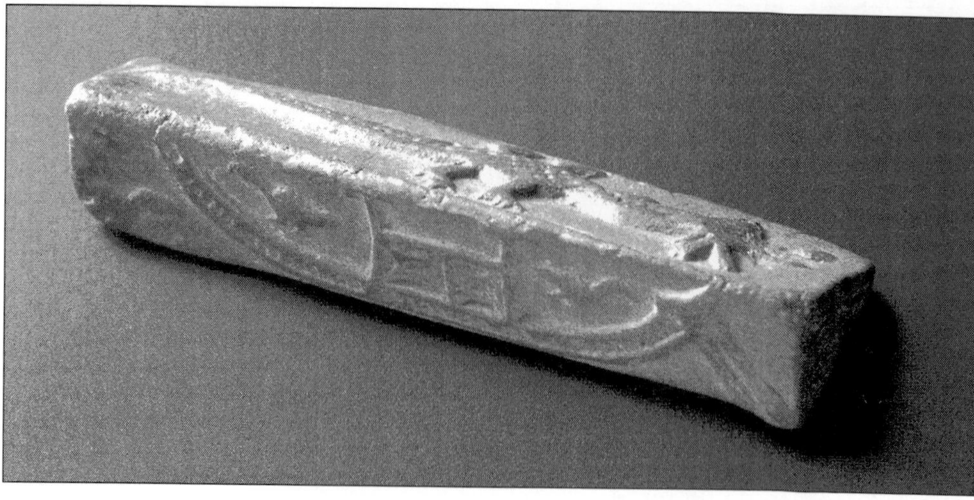

Fig. 7.24. Mohenjo-daro: Depiction of boat.

opened up. Thus, during the Mature Harappan stage, the trade expanded to the other civilisations. A seal from Mohenjo-daro depicting a boat is at Fig. 7.24.

Land route was used for transportation in a landlocked area. Items of natural wealth were first moved to the places of manufacture. From the places of manufacture, which were located in larger cities and in proximity to the area where raw materials were available, the finished goods were then sent out to smaller cities. Items that were traded were grains, raw materials, finished products and would have included wares and ornaments. Agate and carnelian was transported from Ratnapur mines, south of Narmada river, to Sindh where bead manufacture took place. Gold dust was dispatched from the Indus area to all the places where gold ornaments were found. Shells were obviously transported from sea coast to their places of manufacture and thence on to the cities. Other notable items were seals, chert weights, shell industry and metallic objects.

Externally, the present-day Iraq, where flourished the Mesopotamian Civilisation in the third millennium BCE, has a lot to offer as a proof of trade contacts between the two civilisations. These sites were spread across the then Mesopotamia, notable

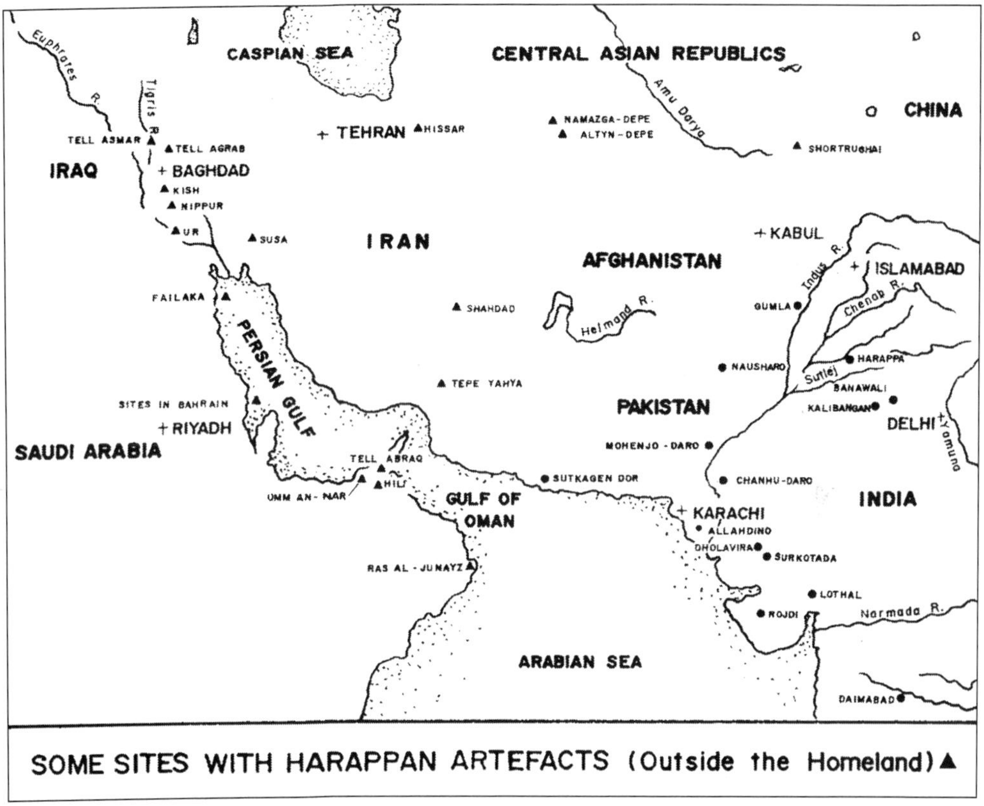

Fig. 7.25. Harappan artefacts outside of India.

amongst them being Tell Asmar, Tell Agrab, Kish, Nippur and Ur. Fig. 7.25 shows the presence of Harappan artefacts in civilisations other than the Indus-Sarasvati Civilisation.

Trade with Mesopotamia was at its peak in the mid-third millennium BCE. In the city of Ur, at many burials of the royalty, carnelian beads from Indus were discovered. Some beads had a drilling technique that was patented, so to speak, by the Indus craftsmen; however, some beads were drilled in a manner that was not to be found in the Indus. These findings led the experts to believe that Mesopotamia must have had the presence of Indus craftsmen in that civilisation.

Fig. 7.26. Bahrain: Harappan seal.

An item typical of the Harappan Civilisation, the dice marked with 1 to 6 dots, has also been found at sites in Mesopotamia.

In the Persian Gulf region, there were contacts with the island of Failaka, the state of Bahrain and Oman. Seals, weights that correspond to Harappan weights, carnelian beads and potteries with motifs of peepal leaf and peacock were common features between the two civilisations. A sample of seal found in Bahrain is at Fig. 7.26. Interestingly, it was a team of archaeologists from India that had excavated a few selected sites in Bahrain in the year 1984-85.

Oman has given evidence of substantial trade with Indus Civilisation which seems to have peaked in the late third millennium BCE. There are enough Indus artefacts in Oman to confirm that. These include beads, ivory items and chert weights as used in the Indus.

Sites in Iran are more inland than near the coast indicating that the trade that existed was through the land route rather than the sea route. Etched carnelian beads were the most common find, others being seals with bull and one with Harappan script.

Turkmenistan and Afghanistan have yielded rich finds that have confirmed trade between these countries and the Harappan Civilisation.

Trade, therefore, between the Harappan Civilisation and Mesopotamia, running through Afghanistan, Turkmenistan, Iran, Oman and Bahrain, is easily understandable due continuity of land and sea route. All these places are like beads in a string stretching from Indian Civilisation up to the Mesopotamian.

With Egypt, there appears to be no direct contact between the two civilisations.

WEIGHTS AND MEASURES

The Harappans' trade was not just barter. Commodities were weighed 5000 years ago also. The Harappan weights were cubical in shape. They were made from chert. If we see the Table below and Fig. 7.27, we realise how methodical the whole system must have been. The following table on Indus weights was made by Hemmy who put them down in the ratios shown:

Mean Wt in gms	Ratio	Mean Wt in gms	Ratio
0.871	1	174.50	200
1.770	2	271.33	320
2.285	8/3	546.70	640
3.434	4	1417.5	1600
6.829	8	2710.4	3200
13.731	16	5556.0	6400
27.405	32	6903.0	8000
54.359	64	10865.0	12800
136.02	160		

It can be seen that the ratios up to 64 were in binary form and after 160, differently. If someone tries to calculate the exact ratios

Fig. 7.27. Chert weights, Dholavira.

in grams, he might observe that there is a bit of an anomaly in ratios vis-à-vis the weight. This has perhaps happened because of wear and tear over a period of time.

Notice that we are seeing weights in the region of 0.87 of a gram! Don't we go into these small values of weight when we buy gold and other precious commodities?

Two points are worth noting. The weights were common throughout the civilisation which spanned over a million square kilometres. Secondly, no changes took place in 700-800 years. This indeed speaks volumes about their standardisation methods. Remember the street widths and the ratios of bricks' length, breadth and thickness.

Insofar as measuring liquids is concerned, no object as such has been discovered.

Four scales, albeit broken, have been found for measurement of length, one each having been discovered at Harappa, Mohenjo-daro, Kalibangan and Lothal. The material used for scales is not standard and is of ivory, shell, bronze and clay. How the last one survived and was discovered speaks volumes about the technical ability of archaeologists to excavate the past! Remember the discovery of the oldest ploughed field at Kalibangan where the furrows were clearly discernible!

The scale at Fig. 7.28, broken at both ends, was made of shell and was discovered at Mohenjo-daro. There were nine graduations. On one of the graduations, there was a hollow circle and on the fifth therefrom, a black dot. Distance between two

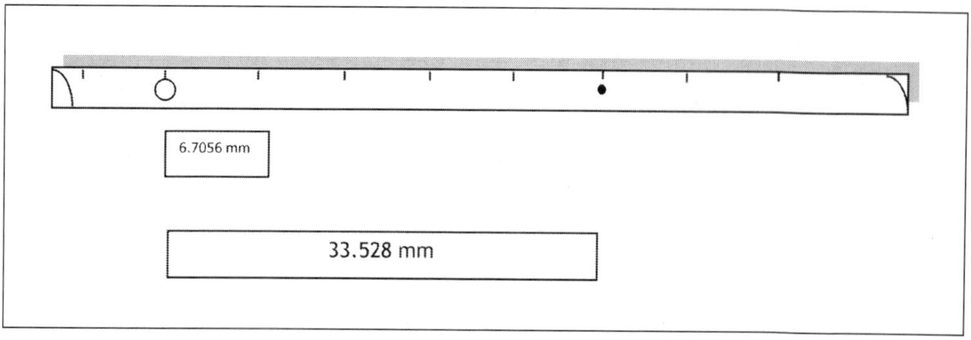

Fig. 7.28. Replica of scale discovered at Mohenjo-daro.

graduations is 6.7056 mms and the distance from the hollow circle to the solid dot is 33.528 mms. If there existed a decimal system as we have seen in weights, then 100 graduations would have meant that the length would have been 670 mms.

Very surprisingly, there appears to have been no standardisation of scales. Those of Lothal, made of ivory, or Harappa, made of bronze, bear no semblance in terms of distance between graduations when compared to the one found at Mohenjo-daro.

RELIGION

Religion during the period can only be inferred since there is, of course, no written record and the seals bearing Indus characters cannot be read as the script itself is not deciphered. One then has to extrapolate the seals, the terracotta figurines and the excavated sites to come to a conclusion.

Recall the story of *Mahishamardini, mahisha* meaning 'buffalo' and *mardini* meaning 'slayer'. *Mahishamardini* is another *avatar* of goddess 'Durga' and the tale has it that the goddess killed the buffalo demon *Mahishasura*. Fig. 7.29 is a terracotta tablet found in Harappa showing the killing of a buffalo in front of a deity.

Fig. 7.29. Harappa: Killing of a buffalo to please deity. (Pl. 12)

Fig. 7.30. Śiva as *Paśupati.*

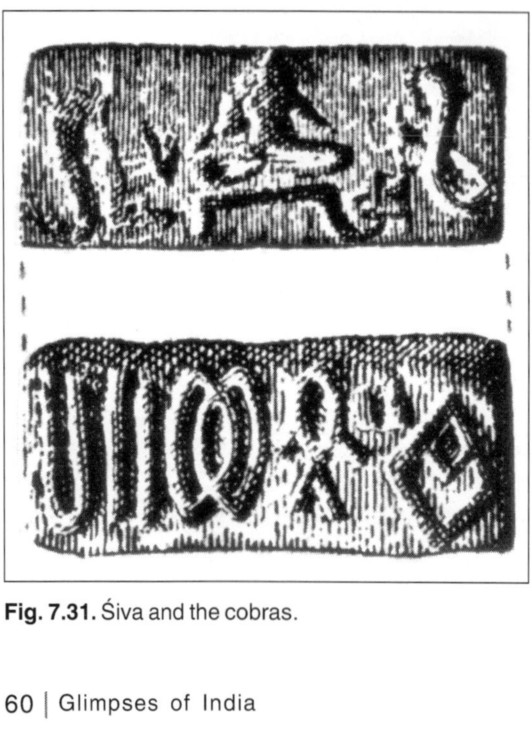

Fig. 7.31. Śiva and the cobras.

A statuette found at Harappa shows a nude male in a dance form, reminding one of Śiva's *Natarāja* pose. There are other seals which depict Śiva. See Fig. 7.30 which shows a seated figure surrounded by animals. A tiger, buffalo, rhinoceros and an elephant can easily be identified. This seal, also found at Harappa, is corroborated by many writers on the subject to be that of Śiva in his *Paśupati* form. Fig. 7.31 is another seal that depicts a figure seated with cobras on either side. Śiva's association with serpents is well known even today; he wears one.

As if to dispel any doubts about Śiva worship, a *liṅga*-cum-*yoni* was discovered at Kalibangan. See Fig. 7.32.

The sculpture of a 'priest in meditation', with eyes closed (Fig. 7.9 earlier) is another sign that it relates to religion during the period.

Peepal tree has been considered sacred since in a few seals it has been associated with deities. So is the 'Swastika', more of which will be discussed later.

That religion was also related to fire and animal sacrifice can be inferred from fire-altars found in Kalibangan. Seven such altars were found in a line in the Citadel. Not far away was a sacrificial pit containing bones of an animal. The Lower Town, too, had fire-altars in most of the houses. Apart from Kalibangan, more altars were discovered in Lothal along with sacrificial pits, and altars at Banawali and Rakhigarhi. No fire-altars were found in the sites of Indus valley, but only in the Rajasthan and Gujarat area. That fire-altars are not to be confused with cooking hearths *rectifies* the western approach that fire-associated rituals were not an ingredient of the civilisation.

Fig. 7.32. Śiva *liṅga*-cum-*yoni.*

THE INDUS SCRIPT

Scripts are broadly divisible into four categories. They are: (a) pictorial, in which a message is sought to be communicated by means of pictures; (b) logographic, in which each sign represents a word; (c) syllabic, in which each sign represents a phonetic value which may comprise one or more consonants with a vowel; and (d) alphabetic, where each sign stands for a sound.

It will be evident that in pictorial script, there would be as many pictures as there would be thoughts; in other words, there would be no limit to the pictures. In the logographic script too, the number of signs would be large since each word is represented by a separate sign. To give an example, the Chinese had a logographic script that had over 50,000 signs at a point in time. In a syllabic script, the number of signs drops considerably. The Egyptian and Sumerian script had about 600 pictorial signs, reducing to 150 as it grew syllabic in nature. As we go alphabetic, the numbers drop considerably: the English language has 26 alphabets and the Devanagari, 48. Some scripts were combination of logos and syllables.

Fig. 7.33. Inscribed potsherd, Kalibangan.

In case of the Indus Civilsation, the script, per se, is gleaned from what has been written on the pots and what has been found on the seals, sealings, copper tablets and metallic objects. The number of such inscribed objects that have been discovered is about 4,000. From these objects, about 400 plus have been identified as signs having their own identity, that is to say the script had over 400 logos and syllables and these were used in combination. These were standardised across the whole of civilisation, from the Indus valley to the Sarasvati valley, over a million and a half square kilometres. An example each of script on a potsherd and on a seal is placed at Figs. 7.33 and 7.34 respectively.

The script, notwithstanding claims made by some of the scholars who made attempts to decipher it, is not considered as having being deciphered. In fact, the effort to decipher it has been worldwide but it has not produced a version that may be accepted by all. The direction of writing was debated too, but was put to rest by B.B. Lal in his paper presented at the International Conference on Asian Archaeology in 1961 when he showed that the writing was from right to left and when the inscription was large, the next line followed the first from left to right. This has since been accepted internationally.

There are two schools of thought on the language of the script. One believes it to be proto-Dravidian and the other, proto-Sanskrit. ('proto' in this context means 'in the earliest form'). Quite evidently, the proto-Dravidian group believes that the Aryan invasion did take place and the Dravidians who were evicted to the south were the original inhabitants of the civilisation and hence, the language has to be Dravidian. The proto-Sanskrit group believes that the Harappans were never invaded and their language of the era was Sanskrit, as in the *Ṛigveda*. What is interesting is that while we can accept that the Dravidianists and the Sanskritists do not accept each other's views, there is a difference of opinion within each group itself. However, it would be too technical to go into details of various approaches and arguments.

Fig. 7.34. Script on seals.

BURIAL PRACTICES

Initially, there was no trace of cemeteries at either Harappa or Mohenjo-daro. The first discovery was at Harappa when excavations recommenced fifteen years later. Thereafter came the discoveries at Lothal and Kalibangan.

At Harappa, there were two cemeteries. In one cemetery, 196 burials were found, all lying north-south. The burials yielded a number of pots and jewellery. While some of the pots are believed to have contained items of food for afterlife, the ornaments were personal in nature. These included bangles, rings, necklaces, and earrings.

With a large population, the number of burials seems small. Scholars think that the burials could have been of a limited group, perhaps the higher hierarchy. The disposal of the dead could have been by other means too.

There is an instance, at Harappa, where the body was put in a coffin of rosewood and deodar.

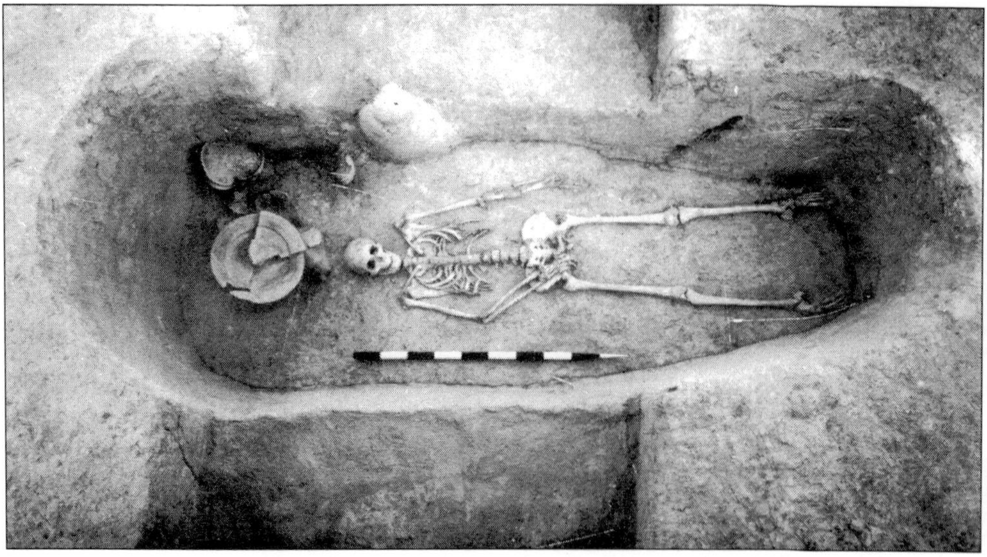

Fig. 7.35. Type I Burial, Kalibangan.

Fig. 7.36. Type II Burial, Kalibangan.

Surprisingly, at Mohenjo-daro, no cemetery was discovered. What has been found are the skeletal remains, full or partial, scattered across areas at various stratigraphic levels. There are indications of injury on the bones, some of which had healed. This led earlier scholars to believe that the Aryans who invaded the civilisation carried out the massacre, a theory that has been proved erroneous. There was no Aryan invasion as theorised in the first half on the twentieth century, and a number of Indian and western scholars have written books debunking this theory.

At Kalibangan three types of burials have been found. Type I burial, rectangular in shape, contained extended human body oriented north-south with the head to the north. Alongside were also interred a large number of pots and a few other objects. Type II burial was without the body but with many pots. The pit appears to have remained exposed, as indicated by the accumulation of bands of sand and clay in it. Type III burial was in a circular or an oval pit, once again with no body but with a large number of pots amongst which there invariably was a large jar. This could have

Fig. 7.37. Type III Burial, Kalibangan.

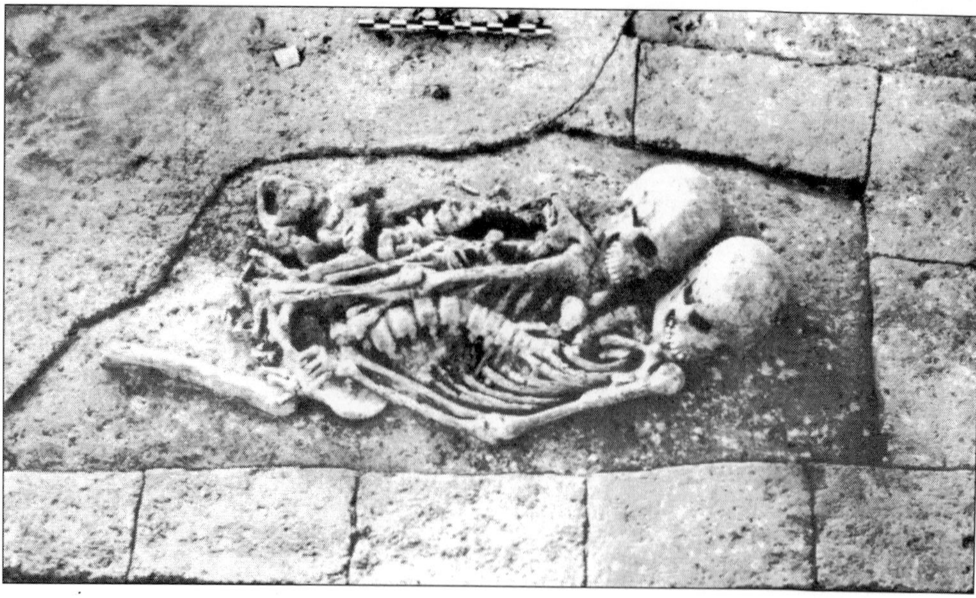

Fig. 7.38. Burial with two skeletons, Lothal.

been the urn pot. However, no remnants of ash or charred bones were discovered in it. See Figs. 7.35 to 7.37.

An interesting point to note is that only Type I burials were found at Harappa, i.e. in the Indus Valley. In the Sarasvati valley, the burials that were discovered were of all types.

Burials at Lothal were unique in that there were instances where a single burial pit had two bodies. Though all the experts do not agree about the identification of the sex of these bodies, some do think that one was a male and the other a female. If that be so, could it be that *sati* was practiced during the Harappan times? See Fig. 7.38.

An interesting burial was found at Kalibangan. It was that of a child having a disproportionately large head, with three holes drilled in it. Obviously, this was a case in which fluid in the brain had to be drained out.

Some more on burials when we discuss Rakhigarhi.

Famous Towns of the Period 8

TOWN: HARAPPA

Excavated by Daya Ram Sahni (1921)
followed by Madho Swarup Vats (1940)
and R.H.Meadow and J.M. Kenoyer (1986 ff.)

As we know, Chandigarh was planned in a grid pattern. Jaipur too, when planned in 1728, was also in a grid pattern. Sisupalgarh near Bhubaneswar in Odisha was planned in a similar pattern in the fourth-fifth century BCE.

Harappans planned it that way some 5000 years ago!

Harappa is in Sahiwal district of Punjab, Pakistan. It is situated by the left bank of river Ravi. The site was about 100 ha or about 250 acres in area. Its perimeter measured six kilometres. The earliest occupation appears to be in the period 3300-2800 BCE. Its occupation had been unbroken, starting from the period mentioned right up to the first half of second millennium BCE. It means that the occupation lasted over a millennium and has been through the Early, Mature and Late Harappan periods.

Major excavations commencing in 1921, spanning over two decades, albeit interspersed, have taken place at Harappa. These were then followed up in 1946 and, again, in 1990s.

Fig. 8.1. Sites with Mature/Late Harappan remains.

It is noteworthy that the Harappan Civilisation in the Indus Valley, Sarasvati basin and Gujarat excelled in terms of town planning, the civilisations of Egypt and Mesopotamia. The latter civilisations had no town planning per se. In most of the Harappan towns, the streets were oriented north-south and east-west. Harappans had living quarters made with bricks. Harappa had all the features of Early and Mature Harappan period. Ascribable to the Mature Period there were an impressive Citadel, a granary, workmen's quarters and the Lower Town, the last of which lay to the south-east of the Citadel. See Fig. 8.2.

The Citadel at Harappa was in the form of a parallelogram, quite unlike the rectangles and east-west north-south planning. It lay 415 m in the north-south direction and 195 m in the east-west. The fortification wall was a massive 13.5 m at base, tapering upwards. Towards east of the Citadel, there were two mounds, each with its own fortification walls. It was on the first mound towards east of Citadel that the Lower town lay. The perimeter wall on the southern side is about 250m long with base of about seven m, and made of bricks measuring 16"x8"x4", once again in the set ratio.

Why so many perimeter walls? Experts feel that it had nothing to do with preparations of any enemy intrusion, since there was no evidence of battle or damage thereof. Most probably each unit had a separate task.

To the north of the Citadel lay the workmen's quarters, pounding platforms and the granary.

The workmen's quarters were within a compound and lay in east-west direction in two rows. The northern block was separated from the southern block by a lane. Each workman's unit was 17 m in depth and 7 m in width. It had two sections, the one in front was a courtyard and the one at rear was a room. Notice the angled entry to the unit in Fig. 8.2, perhaps to ensure privacy.

Further north were the pounding platforms. Eighteen units can be seen and these were circular in shape. Each unit was ten feet in diameter and at the surface level was ringed by a single row of wedge-shaped bricks.

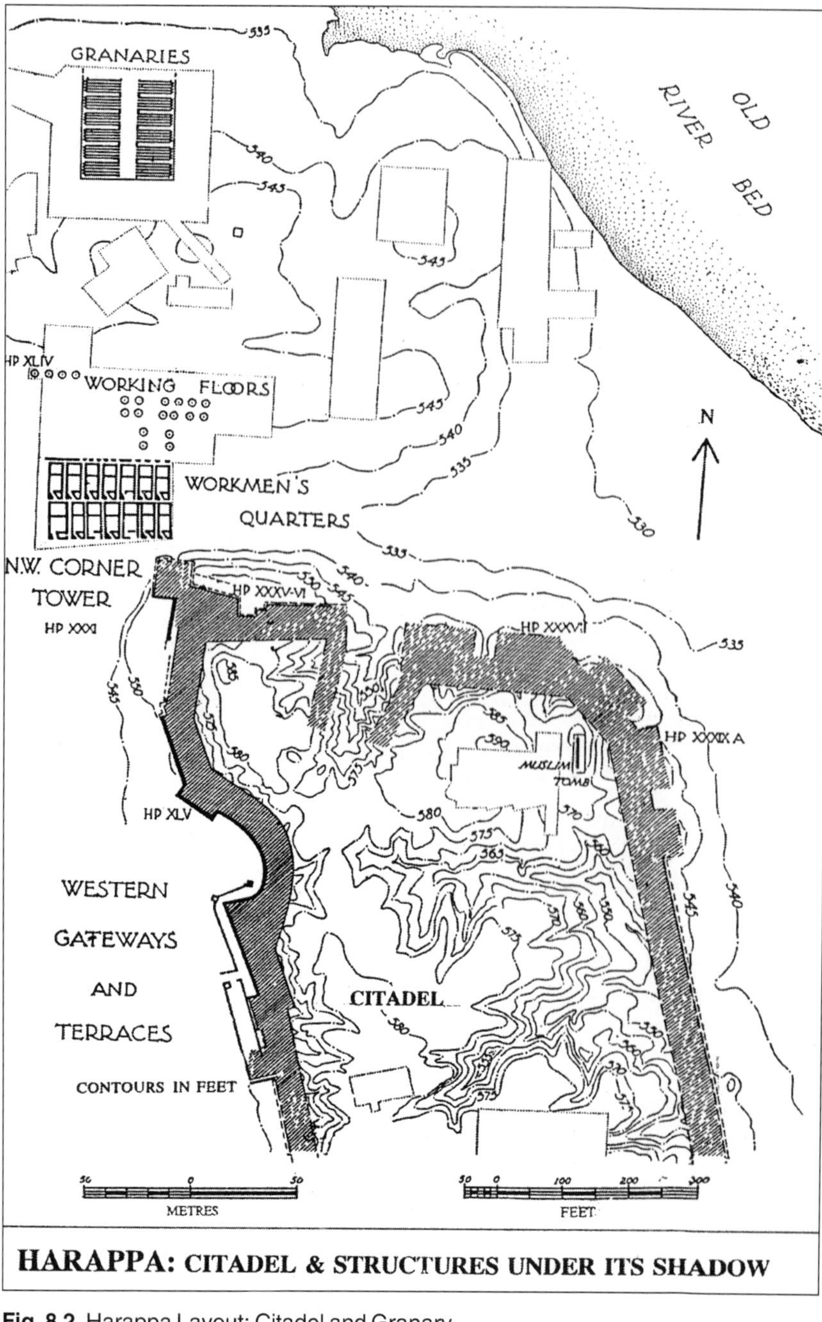

Fig. 8.2. Harappa Layout: Citadel and Granary.

In the centre of each unit there was a hollow in which were found husked remnants of barley and straw. This gave rise to the deduction that these were platforms for pounding grains. Also notice the location of the pounding floors, just next to the granary!

A word about the granary. Fig. 8.3 shows the layout. The granary had an eastern block and a western block. The blocks were separated by a central aisle, seven meters wide. Each block had six units, each measuring 15x6 m. These were the rooms in which the grains were stored. There existed a passage for air to flow into these rooms in order to prevent stale air from degrading the quality of grains.

For constructing the buildings at Harappa both mud bricks and baked bricks were used. The bricks were in the ratio 4:2:1:: length: breadth: thickness and this did not vary. The floors of the buildings were usually of mud but in some cases bricks were used. Sometimes charcoal was embedded in the floor to ensure that termites were taken care of, and moisture absorbed. The bathing

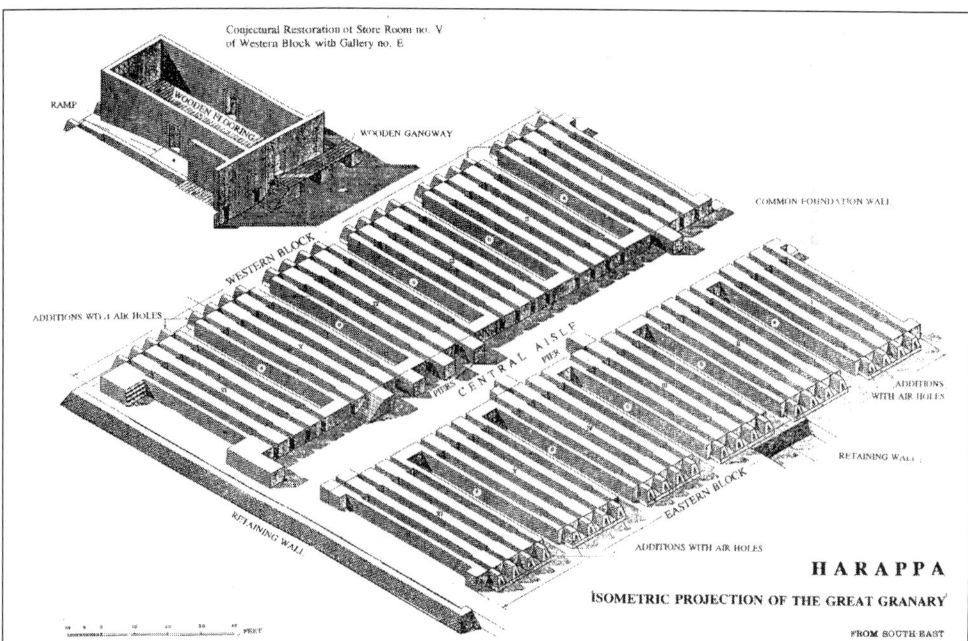

Fig. 8.3. Harappa: Granary.

area was made of baked bricks or stone as were the drains. A typical house consisted of a central courtyard with living rooms surrounding it. The main entry/exit was not towards the main street but towards the side lanes. Two storied houses were not uncommon. The stairs in many houses indicate a double-storied accommodation.

Sheesham and deodar were used for doors and furniture.

There were standard weights, measures and seals. Different seals were used, perhaps to identify recipient or the sender. Agriculture was the main source of economy and trade. Cotton was the main export item.

Pottery was wheel-made, just as we can see today and what we call potter's wheel. Animals were domesticated.

TOWN: MOHENJO-DARO

Excavated by RD Banerji (1922)
John Marshall (1931 ff.)
And EJH Mackay (1938 ff.)

Mohenjo-daro is located in Larkana district of Sindh, Pakistan. Its literal translation is 'city of the dead'. Built in the Mature Harappan period, it is dated back to 2600 BCE and appears to have lasted seven centuries, its decline commencing in 1900 BCE. It had been constructed when the Harappan Civilisation was already blooming or had been evolved. In other words, the knowhow of laying a city and the culture of the period had already made a mark.

Mohenjo-daro is one of the largest cities of the Harappan Civilisation, the overall perimeter being five km. The city was carefully planned: the streets, as usual, running north-south and east-west. Parallel to the major streets there were minor ones, resulting in smaller blocks in which residential houses were constructed. Thus all streets cut each other at right angles. The major streets were 9m wide and the lanes 1.5m.

The city had a Citadel and to its east, the Lower Town. See Fig. 8.4. The Citadel itself measures 380m north-south and 190m east-west and is on a mud brick platform 12m higher than ground

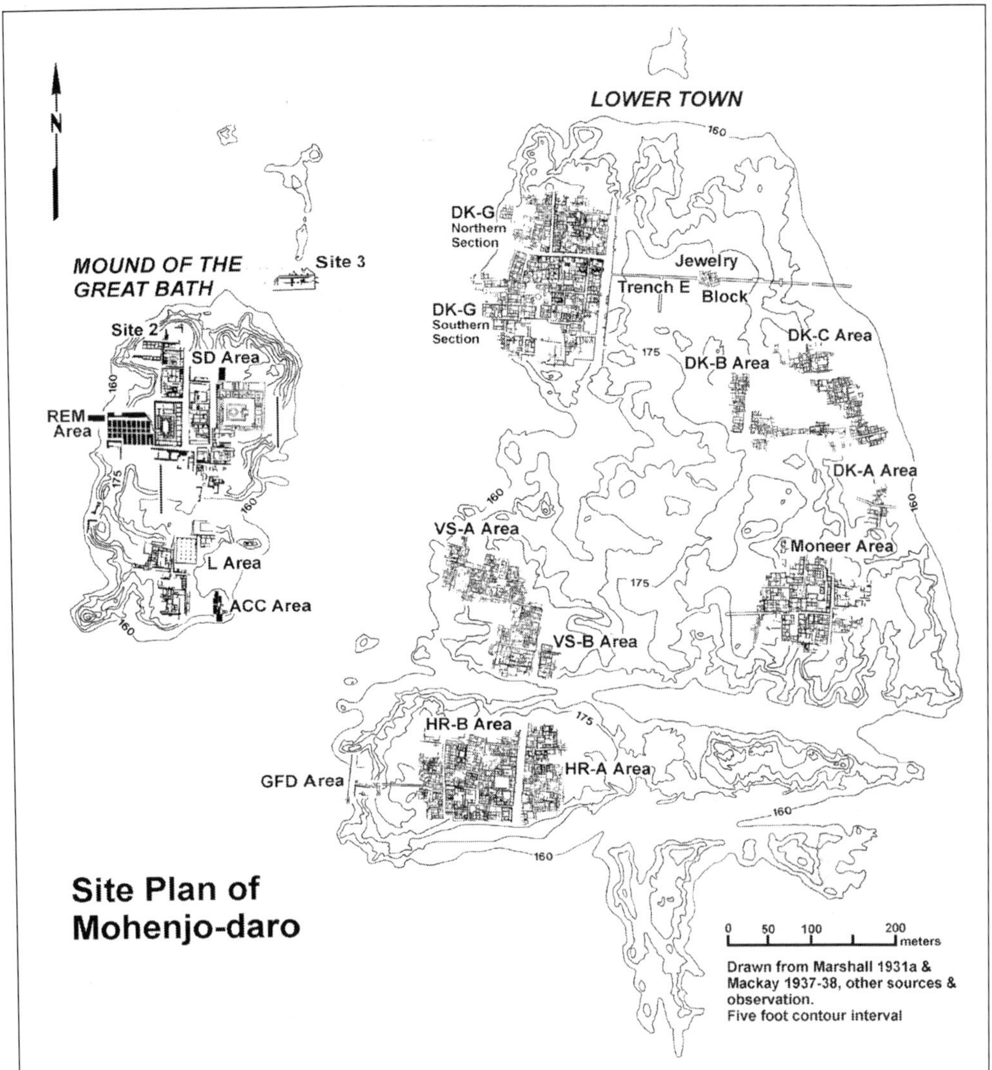

Fig. 8.4. Mohenjo-daro: Site plan.

level. This 2:1 ratio is the same as what we saw at Harappa. Within the Citadel there are a 'bath', a granary and an assembly hall.

Fig. 8.5 shows the 'The Great Bath' as it was aptly termed for its planning, given the vintage, and it being the first such public

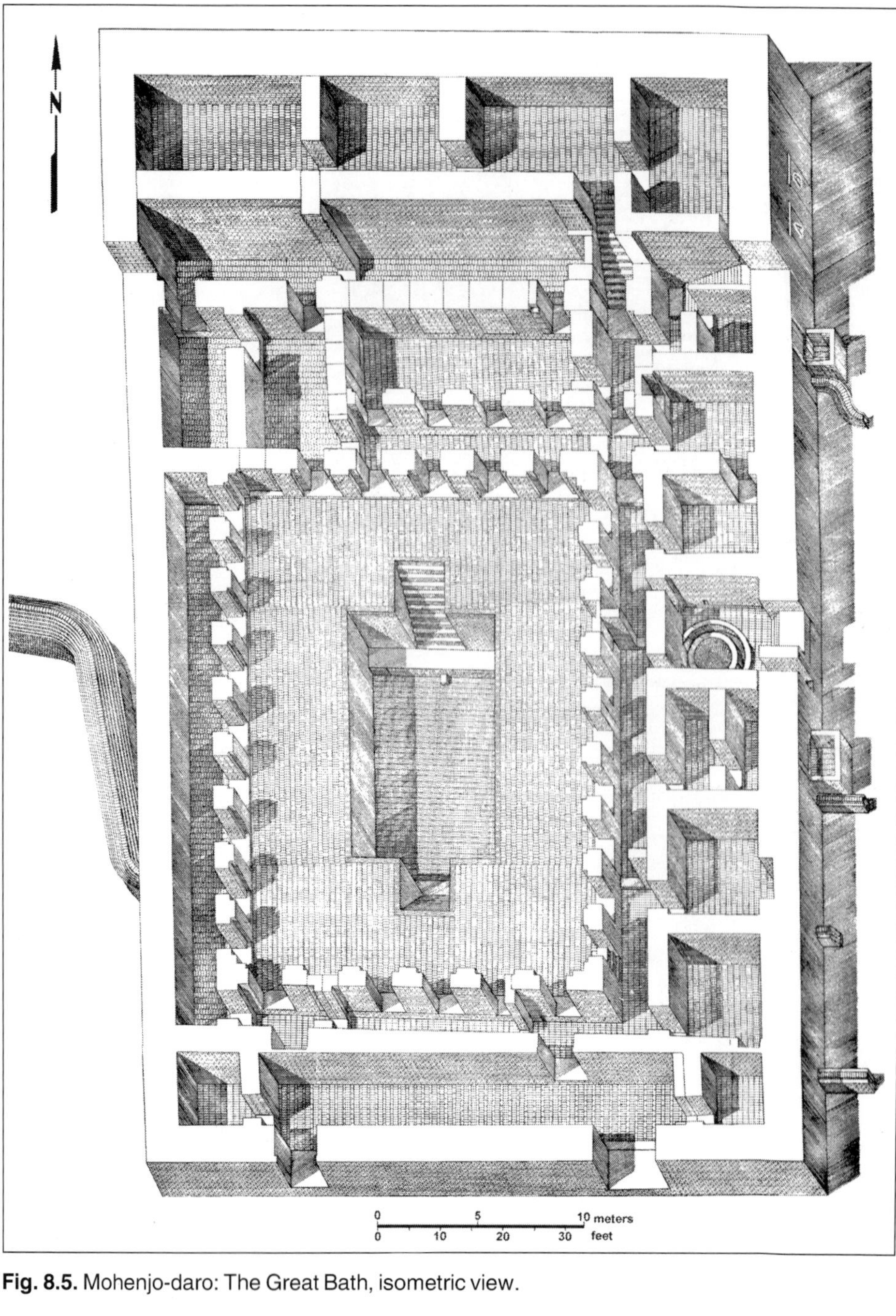

Fig. 8.5. Mohenjo-daro: The Great Bath, isometric view.

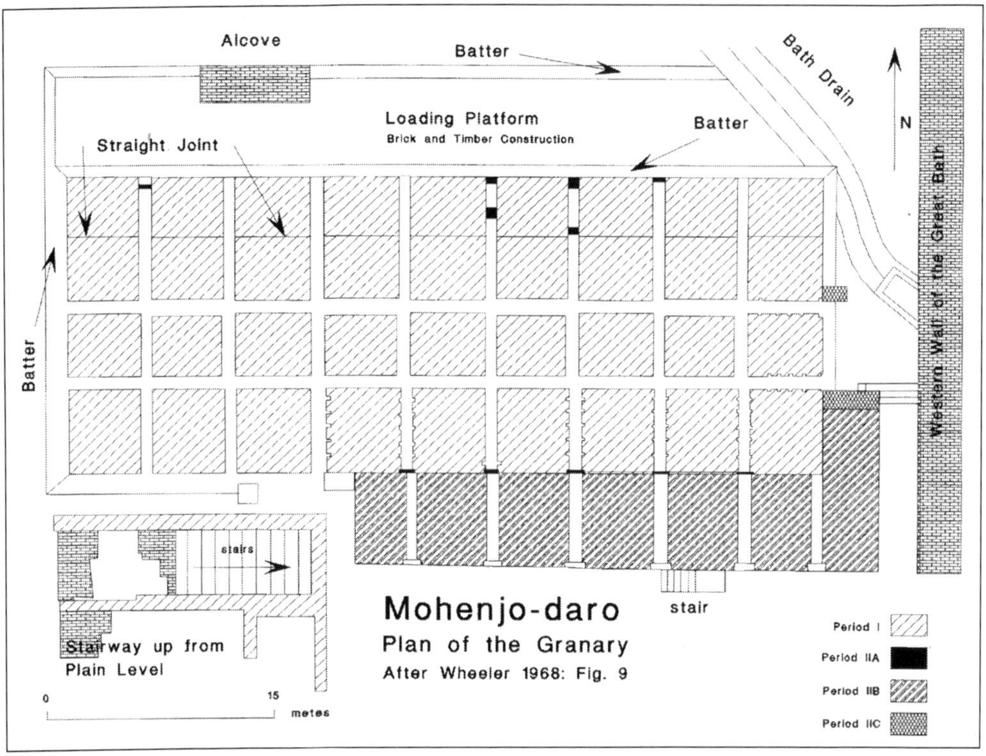

Fig. 8.6. Mohenjo-daro: Granary.

bath anywhere in contemporary civilisations in the world. The bath, which could as well be a swimming pool of today, was 11.7 x 6.9m with a depth of 2.4m. Two staircases, one to the north and the other to the south, led to the floor of the bath. It was kept water-tight by use of gypsum mortar on the floor and on the first side wall. Behind the first side wall stood the second side wall and between the two walls was damp-proof bitumen! So much for prevention of leakage. The water was drained out by a single drain which was constructed on the south-west of the bath.

By the side of the bath, there were corridors. And after that, there were several rooms, one of which contained a well. This must have been used for providing water to the bath. In the north of the bath there were eight rooms which were in fact bathrooms with staircases leading to the second floor. It is believed that the rooms in the upper floor were residences of priests who could come down the stairs for proceeding to the 'great bath'.

The granary was built on a brick platform, 50m east-west and 27 m north-south. The granary itself measured 45 x 22.5 m. It had twenty-seven square and rectangular blocks, arranged in three rows of nine each. These lay east-west. Each block was separated by the other by a passage. Most likely, on these blocks there stood a superstructure of wood. On the southern side of the granary was a staircase from ground level to the granary level. On the granary's north was a loading platform reaching up to the same level as the granary. Towards north-west of the platform was an alcove to allow the bullock carts to come up from where the grain could be off-loaded.

The Lower Town had two major north-south and two east-west streets dividing it into nine sectors. Each sector was subdivided into house-blocks by lanes. The streets had drainage systems with manholes at regular intervals.

Sanitation was accorded an extremely high priority as is evident in the planning. Drainage system included horizontal and vertical drains, and drains and soak pits along the streets. Main drains ran below the major streets and larger lanes. Inspection traps were discovered at regular intervals. Drains from houses ran out to meet the street drains.

The sizes of houses varied. The large houses were 75m across with two courtyards. Both courtyards had rooms around them. Some buildings had two stories.

Within the township, there were shops and workshops for potters, bead-makers, shell-workers, coppersmiths, etc.

A number of artefacts were found during the excavations, such as carved seals, copper and stone tools, balances and weights, jewellery, toys and human figures. There are two that deserve special mention and we have seen them earlier. Remember the 'dancing girl' and 'priest in meditation'.

TOWN: KALIBANGAN

Excavated by B.B. Lal and his colleagues (1960-69)

Kalibangan, located in Hanumangarh District of Rajasthan, lies on the left bank of present-day Ghaggar, which has been identified with ancient Sarasvati. Encompassed within a perimeter of about 2 km, the site has three mounds located from west to east. It was the westernmost mound which was occupied during the Pre-Harappan times. This Pre-Harappan settlement was brought to an end by an earthquake around 2700 BCE. After a gap of about a hundred years, the site was re-occupied with full features of Mature Harappan stage. This also resulted in some of the Pre-Harappan features being subsumed in the Mature Harappan occupation.

The excavations relating to the earlier period in the western mound did reveal that the settlement was enclosed by a fortification wall measuring about 250m and 170m in general direction of NS and EW in form of a parallelogram with a certain deviation at the northern wall. The roads followed the direction of the enclosure. Houses were made of mud bricks, the bricks being in the ratio of 3:2:1 as against 4:2:1 of Mature Harappan period. A typical house was centred around a courtyard with rooms by its side. Cooking was done in the courtyard where ovens were installed. The main drain exited from this courtyard and was made with kiln-fired bricks.

Once the site was resurrected a century later in the Mature Harappan period, the new inhabitants built a Citadel on the western mound over the earlier mound (Fig. 8.7). The Citadel was like a rectangle oriented 240m north-south and 120m east-west. It was divided by a medial east-west wall, splitting the rectangle in two squares. The northern square contained residential houses and the southern had many platforms, which were used for rituals. Two important rituals could be identified.

The first one was animal sacrifice and the evidence is the presence of bovine bones and antlers excavated in one of the pits

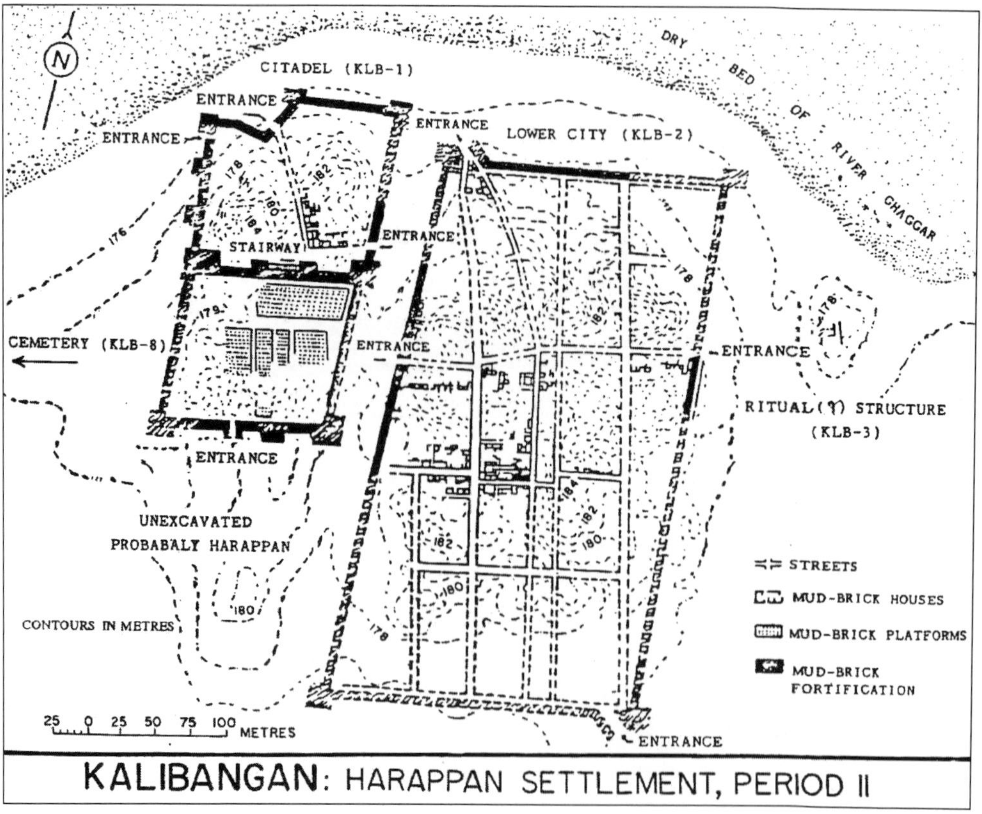

Fig. 8.7. Kalibangan: Site plan, Mature Harappan stage.

(Fig. 8.9). As if to confirm, also found was a terracotta tablet with an engraving that showed an animal with a noose around him being led to the sacrificial altar by a man, with a deity engraved on the other side.

The second ritual was a kind of worship associated with fire. The 'fire-altars'(see Fig. 8.11) that were discovered lay north-south, with a wall to their east. That indicated that the worshippers faced the east, a ritual that is still prevalent today. Also found was a jar containing ashes and charcoal, indicating that the fire was kept burning to be used in the fire-altars. Close to the fire-altars, there were a well and a bathing platform, indicating that a ritual bath was a part of the ceremony.

It becomes evident that the Citadel was a religious centre with the northern half being occupied by the priests. There exists a long passageway joining the northern half to the southern one.

Fig. 8.8. A street in the Lower Town, Mature Harappan.

The Lower Town was to its east on the central mound. It measured 360m x 240m and had fortification walls along its periphery. This town had five north-south and four east-west streets. Their widths were 1.8m, 3.6m, 5.4m and 7.2m, planned in the ratio of 1:2:3:4. Some thought! Normally mud bricks were used and these were in the ratio of 4:2:1, length, breadth and thickness. Sometimes kiln-fired bricks were also used, particularly for drains or where water was involved. Some houses had charcoal floor interspersed with soling of broken hard-fired nodules over which clay was laid out. It is learnt that this kind of flooring is laid out even today in neighbouring villages in order to prevent moisture creeping up the walls and to prevent termites.

The houses comprised a courtyard with living rooms on three sides. The fourth side had the entrance wide enough to bring a bullock cart inside. Some houses had a well in the courtyard. The houses had platforms built by the side of the entrance for people to sit and talk.

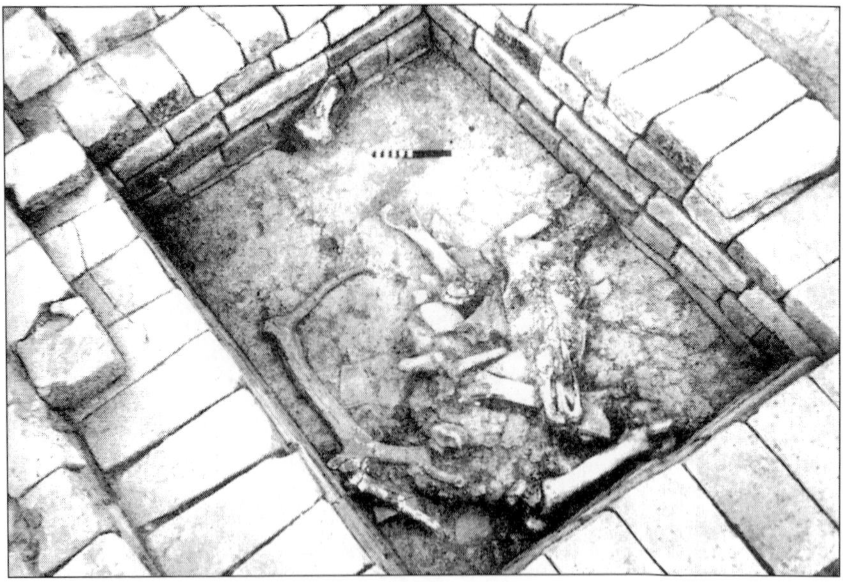

Fig. 8.9. Kalibangan: Brick-lined sacrificial pit.

Fig. 8.10. Kalibangan: Fire-altars.

Fig. 8.11. Kalibangan: A drain discharging into a soakage jar.

Hygiene was maintained at high level. Soakage jars were placed at the end of drains to contain the spread of dirty water. (Fig. 8.12)

The easternmost mound, smallest of them all, contained only fire-altars indicating that this mound was used for ritualistic purposes only. With fire-altars already in the Citadel, were the ones in this mound for commoners?

The most remarkable discovery in Kalibangan was a ploughed agricultural field, to be discussed later.

The decline of Kalibangan in pre-mature stage was due to an earthquake. The shift of earth is evidenced by the faulted stratification as was seen in the Fig. 6.8. In the later stage, i.e. the Mature Harappan stage, the decline was

Fig. 8.12. Kalibangan: Bronze bull. (Pl. 13)

due to the drying up of the Sarasvati river which forced its abandonment.

TOWN: BANAWALI

Excavated by R.S. Bisht in 1980s

Banawali is located in Hissar district of Haryana and lies 120 km upstream from Kalibangan, on the now-dried Sarasvati. The settlement measured about 400m by 400m. It shows all the three cultural periods, viz. Early, Mature and Post-Mature Harappan. There is continuity from Early Harappan to Mature Harappan unlike at Kalibangan. However, there is a break between the Mature and Post-Mature Harappan period.

This town too had fortification walls along its periphery (Fig. 8.13). Within it lay the Citadel, or the Acropolis as the excavator has termed it, and the Lower Town. With the Town's southern fortification wall as its base, the Citadel's fortification wall was built northwards in a semi-ellipse shape. Width of the wall was 18 ft to 21 ft at base! On either side of the wall there ran a street along the wall both on the Citadel side and on the Lower Town side.

A moat was identified adjacent to the eastern face of the fortification-wall of the Lower Town. But excavations were not carried on the other three sides to confirm its presence or continuity of the water channel. The dry bed of the Sarasvati lies only about 200m to the south of the settlement and feeding the water to the moat through a man-made channel would have been no problem. The moat could have served as an extra security system, but whether from floods or from outside attack is not known.

Streets ran north-south and east-west in the Citadel but not so in the Lower Town. The houses followed the usual pattern with a courtyard in the centre and rooms around it. Rooms had a mud-brick floor and the walls had alcoves built into them. The alcoves measured 1mx1m and also 1mx2m. In one of the houses, a wash basin was discovered in the toilet, properly connected to a drain!

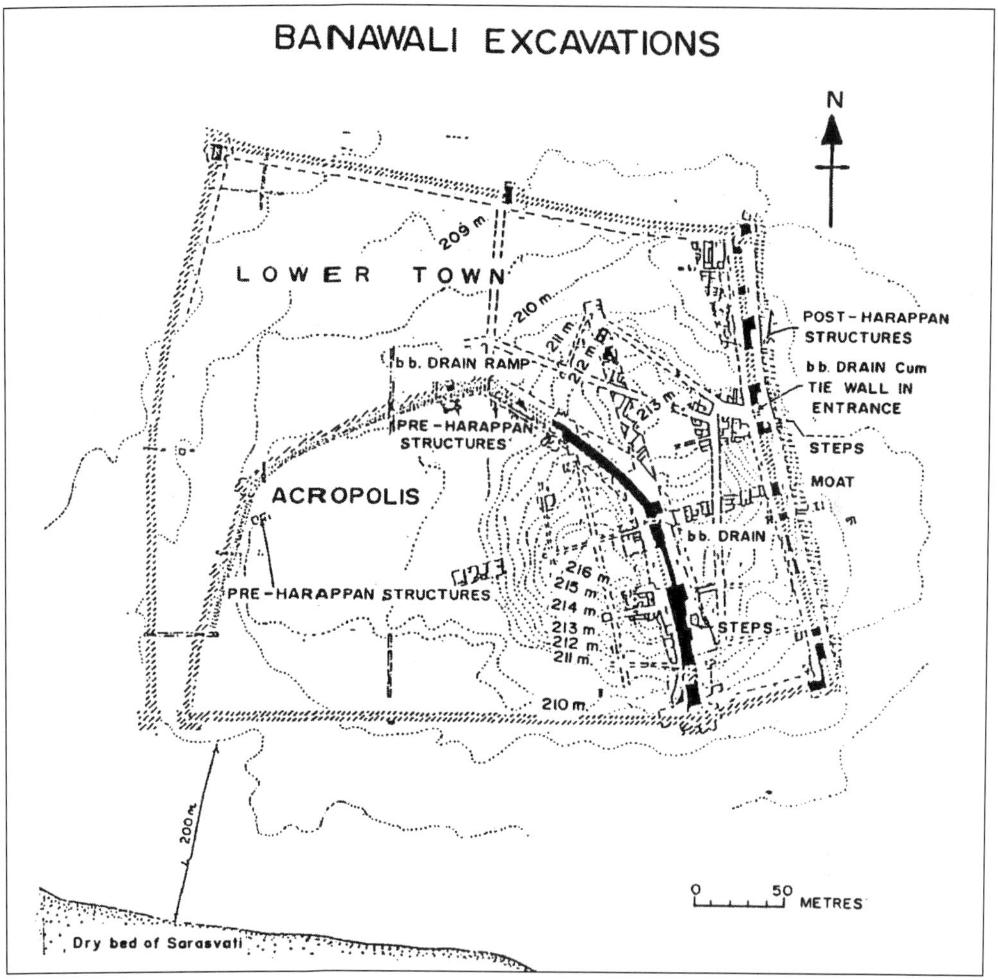

Fig. 8.13. Banawali: Site plan.

Wherever housing was involved, mud bricks were used. Wherever, water was present, kiln-fired bricks were used. It could be drains, wells or baths.

Banawali has yielded a large numbers of antiquities. Quite a few of them have been found in the residential houses. These included copper objects, beads, bangles, seals, sealings and weights. What was new here was the discovery of a large number of beads of lapis lazuli, carnelian and gold. A touchstone bearing

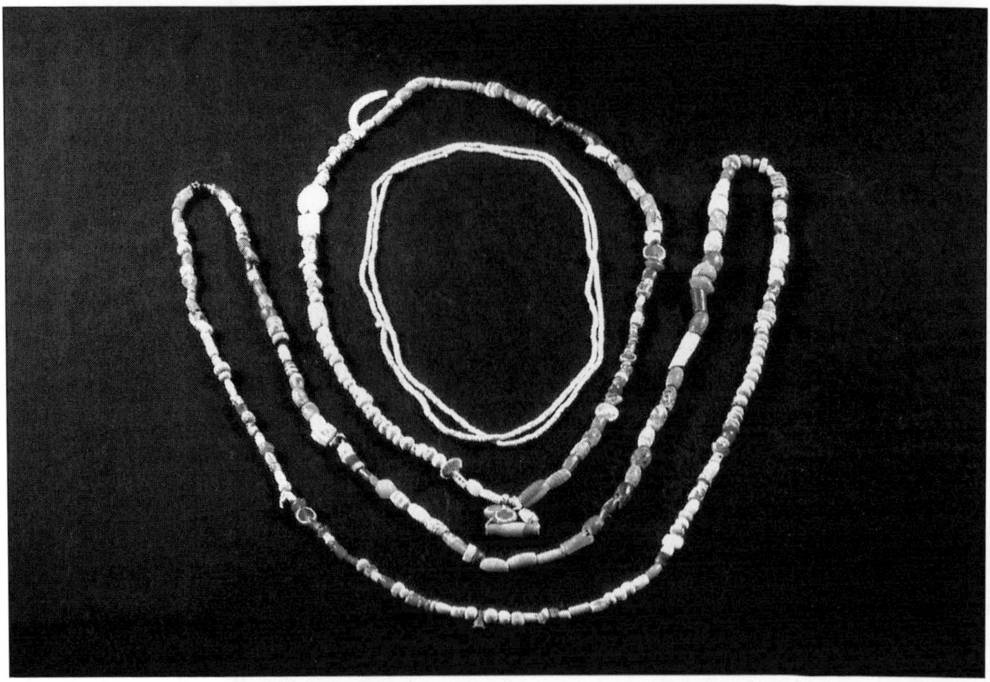

Fig. 8.14. Banawali: Agate-bead necklace. (Pl. 14)

gold streaks of various hues was also discovered suggesting that there existed a practice of checking the purity of gold. Bangles of shell and clay were also discovered.

Fig. 8.15. Banawali: Pot with beads. (Pl. 15)

A terracotta plough was discovered which we shall see later.

Faience ornaments have been found in large quantities. These include rings, earrings, bangles and anklets. It appears that at the time corresponding to the end of Mature period, the faience industry was at its peak.

The type of large houses and the contents found therein suggest that Banawali was inhabited by well-to-do people. A house with lots of seals and weights indicated that it may have belonged to a rich merchant and another one with large quantities of beads of gold, lapis lazuli and carnelian indicated that the resident could have been a rich jeweller!

The decline of Banawali was for the same reasons as that of Kalibangan, viz. the drying up of the river Sarasvati.

TOWN: RAKHIGARHI

Excavated by Amarendra Nath (1997-2000)

Rakhigarhi is located in the Hissar district of Haryana. It is situated on the dry river-bed of ancient Drishadvati, which is now known as Chuttang and is for most part dry. In olden times, the Drishadvati flowed through the modern districts of Karnal, Jind and Hisar before meeting the Sarasvati. Compared to other cities, and that include Harappa and Mohenjo-daro, Rakhigarhi was huge. It covered an area of almost 350 hectares. However, the excavations were limited due to the area being presently occupied and cultivated but the period of its occupation could be established. The excavations indicate that one of the pockets was inhabited even earlier than the Early Harappan phase. This is evidenced by the findings of Hakra wares, the same as were found in Cholistan, Kunal and Bhirrana. The other mounds/pockets continued into the Mature and late Harappan phase. Most are only Mature phase inhabitation.

There are seven mounds at Rakhigarhi. These are numbered from RGR 1 to RGR 7. Out of these mounds, RGR 1, RGR 2 and RGR 6 have revealed occupation by the pre-Harappan inhabitants with RGR 1 continuing through the Mature Harappan days. In other words, the site was occupied in a period that can go back to Kunal days. This shows a continuity of Rakhigarhi dating back from fourth to fifth millennium BCE. Despite the fact that most of the area is not excavated, the findings reveal that there did exist all characteristics of the Harappan Civilisation with artefacts dating back to 5000 years. This was achieved by C-14 dating confirming

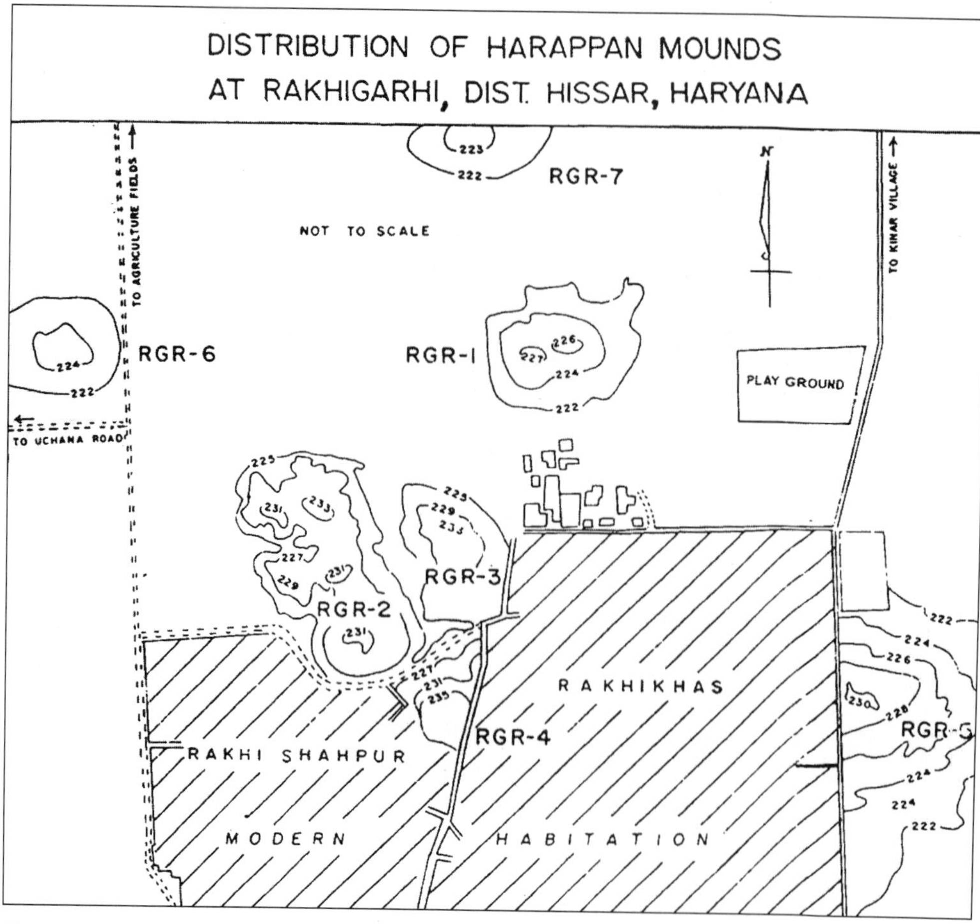

Fig. 8.16. Rakhigarhi: Site plan.

occupation from the Pre-Harappan right through to Mature Harappan stage.

The excavations revealed remains of domesticated cattle, zebu, goat, sheep, buffalo and pigs in area ascribed to have been occupied by the earliest inhabitants. The maximum collection of bones, as can be expected, is from cattle, thus giving us an indication of animal husbandry and, perhaps, of subsistence.

There have been two patterns for growing crops. And they are just the same today! *Rabi* and *Kharif*. *Rabi* crops, grown in winter, have been barley, wheat, peas, lentils, chick pea, etc. The summer or *kharif* crops have been rice, millets, dates, gram, cotton, etc. Recall that other sciences play a role in establishing and supporting or negating evidences and in this archaeo-botany played a major role in establishing the crop-types.

Rakhigarhi had a few settlements around it and these appear to be satellite towns to support the main town. They show up as agricultural lands that provided crops to the 'centre', thus boosting the latter's granaries. An interesting produce of this area has been *bathuā*. We know that *bathuā* is used as a filling in *roṭī*, but it was also used then to extract green colour for dyeing. Its seeds, incidentally, are used for preparation of starch used for stiffening the fabric. The seeds were found in the burnt brick-bat floor of a courtyard which was used as a dyeing vat.

That brings us to 'what were they doing there?'. Textiles, of course! To corroborate this, imprints of fabric over copper ornaments, a burnt patch of textile over a mud floor, besides seeds having been found to have stuck to a vessel! Spindle whorls from pre-Harappan and spools from Mature Harappan levels indicate flourishing textile industry. Evidence of cotton from Kunal further strengthens the view.

Yet another adjacent settlement shows presence of 17 kilns in an area 75 x50 m. Kilns, as we saw earlier, were used to fire clay for making terracotta cakes. The finished product was sent to the main site for export or local use.

What is evident, therefore, is that the satellite towns supported the main site. In the first occupational stages, there was agriculture to support the means of living and as the civilisation progressed, it not only grew in agricultural sector but also introduced material culture for production of artefacts of other metals and semi-precious stones. These raw materials were from outside the area. An example is of quartzite from which querns, polishers, pounders, hammer stones, pestles, etc. were made. Quartzite is not available at Rakhigarhi and the nearest source is in district Bhiwani, 70 kms southwest of Rakhigarhi, the other being Delhi. Copper was brought in from Rajasthan. A large number of copper objects have been discovered in Rakhigarhi.

Gold objects and ornaments have been found and these consist of beads, pendants, rings, coiled springs, etc. Silver and lead objects have also been reported from the site, though their number is small.

Steatite was a popular material of the civilisation and its presence at Rakhigarhi is no exception. Faience-working kiln was also discovered at RGR 2. Bangles and beads are abundant. Agate was exploited by lapidary workers. Most of the beads recovered at site are made of carnelian, which is produced by heating natural agate. Lapis Lazuli is another item found, though small in number. Ivory, too, is in very small number.

Unfortunately, the site has been heavily encroached upon. Notwithstanding, excavations were carried out in the limited area available. The layout of township is similar to the towns of that age. There are well constructed roads, drainage systems, rainwater harvesting and other features that consolidate the opinion that the civilisation was a well governed one.

A granary with mud-brick wall with lower portion containing traces of lime indicate awareness of use of lime as an insecticide.

Rakhigarhi gives a similar insight into the religious practices of Mature Harappan period as does Kalibangan. Sacrificial pits containing bones, horns and hoofs of cattle and goat were found.

At RGR 7, a cemetery was discovered which contained about a dozen graves. Some burials were also found at RGR 1 and 2. The burial practices were in consonance with the times. Earthen wares and ornaments formed the objects that had to be placed with the departed ones, leading one to think, just like the Egyptians, that they believed that there is life after death. The accompaniments consisted of earthen wares that consisted of dish-on-stand, bowl-on-stand, goblets, beakers, vases, etc; ornaments like necklaces, beads, bangles also formed a part of funerary accompaniments. See Fig. 8.17.

There was a distinction between the burials of males and females. The females were offered double the number of earthen wares. A question does arise as to how does one identify the difference between the two skeletons. The most important difference between the two skeletons is found at the pelvis level. In females, the pelvis is low and wider. The pelvic ring is wider and more circular to allow growth of a new born. Due to a wider hip, the second difference shows up in the thigh bones. They become more angular.

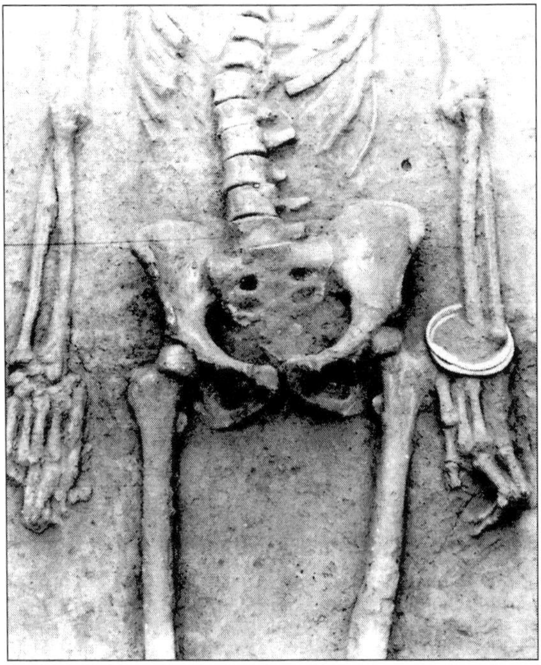

Fig. 8.17. Rakhigarhi burial: Shell bangles on left wrist.

In 2014, excavations at Rakhigarhi were re-started with two very specific aims. The first aim is to establish the nativity or otherwise of the Harappan people. This is being done with the help of South Korean archaeologists who have developed software to build a human form by extracting DNA from skeleton. It is claimed that from the DNA thus obtained, the software can even build a face and body from the skeletal frame. The second aim is to suggest measures to make Rakhigarhi as a tourist spot.

TOWN: LOTHAL

Excavated by SR Rao (1955-62)

Lothal is located in Ahmedabad district of Gujarat. The habited area measures 280m in north-south direction and 225m in the east-west. Set-up of the township, as seen at Fig. 8.18, reflected uniformity with the general planning of those days. Here also, the streets were laid out in cardinal directions, the widest being 12m in width and the narrowest, 3.6m. The houses followed the typical Harappan pattern with a courtyard and rooms on three sides. The inmates were engaged in agricultural and industrial

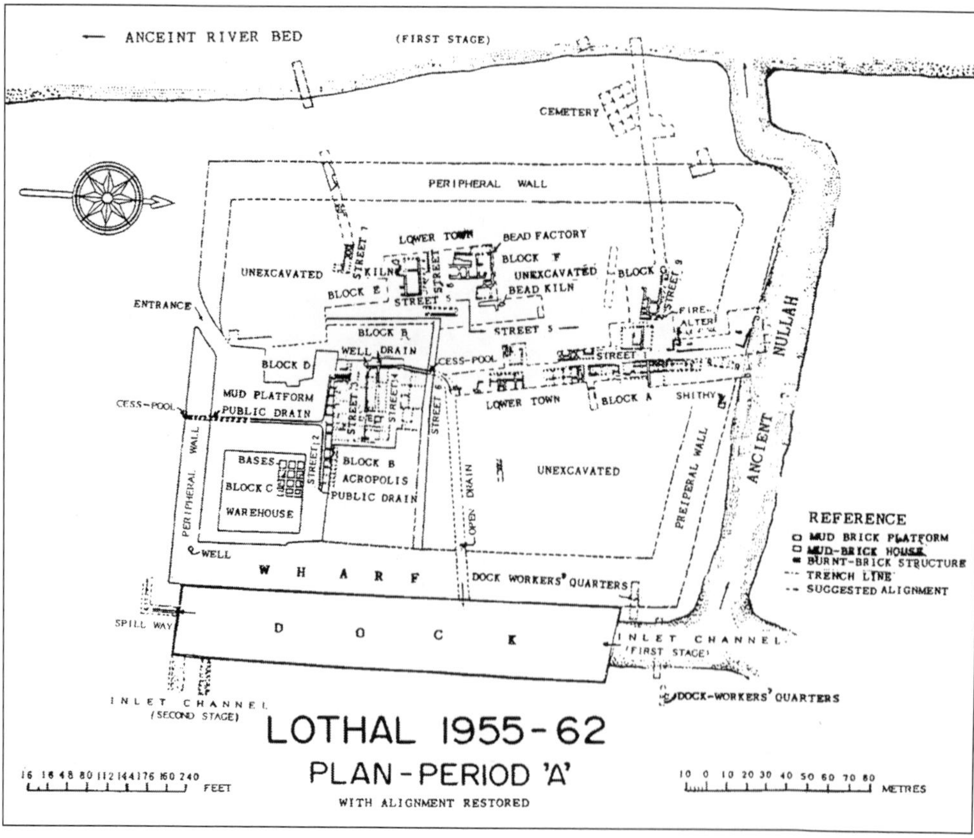

Fig. 8.18. Lothal: Site plan.

activities. The discovery of lots of beads in different stages of manufacture and their raw materials shows that Lothal was a major industrial centre for bead-making. Copper artefacts were manufactured locally. Finds also included an angle-measuring instrument marked at 40 degrees, covering 360 degrees — perhaps used for navigation. The discovery of this angle-measuring instrument, the compass, makes it the earliest in the world.

But the greatest contribution of Lothal is that it has given the world the earliest dockyard, dating back to the third millennium BCE. It was connected through a river to Gulf of Khambhat, an inlet of the Arabian Sea, and was surrounded by retaining walls. It is surmised that during high tides at sea, the

Fig. 8.19. Lothal: Dockyard.

water came up to the dockyard enabling boats to move in and load or offload the cargo. Anchors were made of stone and the goods were unloaded in the nearby wharf. Commodities that were to be loaded were brought in from nearby warehouse and the boats were made ready for sail. Flooding during high tide was offset by an opening in the dockyard which enabled excess water to flow out.

It is interesting to know that a few western scholars, who without giving much thought, and loath to give due credit to the 'first dockyard discovered', have contested the idea of it being a dockyard. They have opined that the said dockyard was indeed a 'tank for storing water'. However, there are arguments that negate the above premise. To name a few, the silt deposited at the bottom of the tank is saline; secondly, there are shells that have been discovered at the bottom of the enclosure; thirdly, 'tank for storing water' was not a necessity since the site contains many wells in the township; and lastly and most importantly, the city drains discharged their water into this enclosure!

There has been a silence thereafter!

The warehouse (Fig. 8.20) was constructed on a mud-brick platform measuring 48 x 40m and 4m high. This high height was to prevent any flooding of the warehouse. On this platform were smaller blocks in rows, each measuring 3.6 x 3.6 x 0.9m and separated by 1.2m-wide passage. When excavated, the passage

Fig. 8.20. Lothal: Warehouse.

was lined with burnt wood and charcoal indicating that it had got burnt. Sixty-five burnt clay seals were found: perhaps, the goods were ready for sail. A lot of material of Indian origin has been found in the excavations in the eastern part of Arabian peninsula, islands in the Persian Gulf and Mesopotamia.

Lothal was a major trade centre. It must also be said in this context that a West Asian seal that has been discovered at Lothal

Fig. 8.21. Lothal: West Asian seal.

indicates maritime trade with that area. Over 200 seals were found during excavation, which is said to be one third of volume of trade in Harappan times. Weights and measures were used to weigh and measure the commodities that were used in trade. Lothal exported gems, beads, shells and ornaments. It is said that the manufacture of beads was so advanced in Lothal that even today, 4500 years later, the same technique is followed in that area. Gold ornaments were popular, especially the five-strand mini gold bead necklace.

A bead-factory has also been identified, with a central courtyard and rooms around it. The courtyard had a raised platform with an anvil. Apart from finished products consisting of many necklaces and fine beads, there were as many unfinished products, raw materials for beads, a drill and other tools. Special furnace for bead-heating was also discovered. Items that were discovered for making beads were opal, carnelian, crystal, jasper, etc.

Citadel, in Lothal, was a part of main township and was not a separate entity as in Kalibangan, Harappa and Mohenjo-daro. However, the Citadel lay on a platform 3.5m high and was about 115m in length and width and consisted of large-sized houses, a well and twelve bathing pavements, each with an inlet and outlet channel, the outlet channel disgorging into a main channel.

The Lower Town was also in north-south direction with streets 6-8m wide. There were residences on either side of streets. The area was used for manufacturing processes. Unfortunately, the structures that comprised residential complex did not survive because of heavy floods, and perhaps that is the reason why the township was abandoned. With the available evidence pertaining to structures, it can be stated that there existed three east-west streets, two east-west lanes three north-south lanes. While the streets were 3 m to 6.5 m in width, the lanes measured 2 m in width. The drainage system survived as an evidence, it being at ground to sub-ground level. The runnels (gutter for effluents) exited from houses, entered lane drains which poured out to discharge into a big cesspool west of citadel. The open drain discharged into the main dockyard. (See Site-plan). The discharge flow was maintained by providing step-down, literally, at frequent intervals.

TOWN: DHOLAVIRA

Discovered by JP Joshi (1968-69)
And excavated by RS Bisht (1989 onwards)

Dholavira is located in the Kutch district of Gujarat and is one of the most prominent and developed sites of this civilisation. It measures about 50 ha. Its occupation began around 2600 BCE and decline came about 2100 BCE. There was a subsequent short-lived re-occupation around 1700 BCE.

The city had three parts: the Citadel, the Middle Town and the Lower town. All had their respective boundary walls yet were within an overall enclosure measuring 770m east-west and 615m north-south. Unlike the other sites, the material used for house construction and fortifications was stone, which is locally available.

The site was occupied beginning with pre-Mature stage. In what was the Citadel area, use of mud bricks in the typical 1:2:4 ratio was found. Evidence of copper was found on crucibles, globules and stone blocks. Some finished products were also discovered. Pottery consisted of fragments of perforated jar and

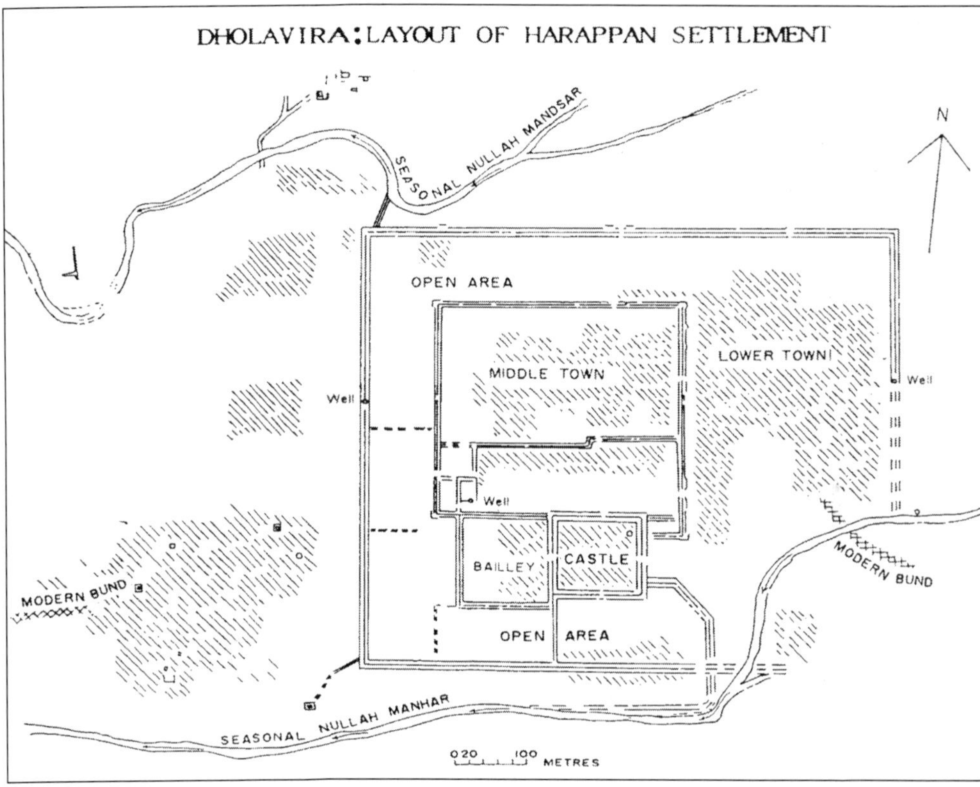

Fig. 8.22. Dholavira: Site plan.

dish-on-stand. Of the Mature stage, there are weights, seals without inscriptions, also seals with inscription and pottery, etc.

The re-occupation shows that the houses were circular on plan and were built in a style different from that of the Mature stage. There appears to be no planning as such and the drainage system had virtually disappeared.

But more on Dholavira of Mature stage: The Citadel complex in the south consisted of two areas, called 'Bailey' and the 'Castle', terms coined by the excavator. The areas were walled but had an interconnection in the form of a gate. Bailey appears to be a residential area since many houses were found there. Castle, on the other hand, had a different purpose. From the interconnecting

Fig. 8.23. Dholavira: Rock-cut reservoir. (Pl. 16)

gate on the west, a street ran along east-west to the eastern end, bifurcating the castle into northern and southern sectors. The composition at the northern end is somewhat unclear but the southern section appears to be a major water related complex.

North of the Citadel there was what could be a stadium, since it is all a plain ground, followed by the Middle Town. Inside the latter, the streets are along cardinal directions. Houses here are large with a courtyard, living rooms and bathrooms. There is a drainage system.

The Lower Town lies to the east of Middle Town. Once again, the streets are in cardinal directions. A lot of stone work has gone into construction of walls, size of the stones being same as that of bricks, 40 x 20 x 10cm. Storage jars, querns and a simple stone mill used for grinding grain by hand were found.

A well with a diameter of 4 m and depth of over 13m was found in the open ground of the castle. Upon water being drawn, it was fed through a channel into a stone-lined tank measuring 4.35 x 2.95 x 3.6 m. However, there were large-sized reservoirs immediately outside the Citadel wall, cut through the basal rock. One of these measures 79m in length and 7m in depth. These reservoirs show how very particular were the inhabitants of Dholavira about water-conservation.

Fig. 8.24. A huge storm-water drain at Dholavira.

In fact, the system of water-supply and its management were the high point of Dholavira. Two seasonal *nullahs* flowed along northwest and southeast of the site. Water from these was harnessed for use of the inhabitants. At least sixteen reservoirs were created. The *nullahs* were dammed to divert water into the reservoirs. Astonishingly, one third of Dholavira was planned for water conservation! Some of the reservoirs were rock-cut.

9 Cultural and Other Continuities

AGRICULTURE: FIELDS AND CROPS

Notice the similarity of fields. The one excavated at Kalibangan in Hanumangarh district of Rajasthan (Fig. 9.1) bears a striking similarity to the one that we see today (Fig. 9.2). The Kalibangan field is ascribable to circa 2800 BCE and belongs to Early Harappan period.

The furrows are dug in north-south and east-west directions. First the east-west furrows are ploughed and then the north-south ones. This is evident in the Kalibangan fields. The distances between the furrows are found to be strikingly similar in the ancient field and the present one. The distance between the north-south furrows is 1.9 meters and that between the east-west is 30 centimetres. This is a typical layout when the farmer is growing two winter crops, viz. those of mustard and gram. The taller of the two crops, the mustard, is sown in north-south direction, and the gram crop sown in east-west direction. With the sun in the southern hemisphere and each furrow 1.9 meters apart, the sun's rays are casting longer shadows northwards which are not impinging on the gram crop!

Agriculture was the backbone of Harappan economy. The Harappan people, apart from mustard and gram, grew wheat,

Fig. 9.1. Kalibangan field as excavated.

Fig. 9.2. Modern-day field.

barley and cotton, to name a few. At least three types of wheat have been identified. Cereals constituted the mainstay in the Indus and Sarasvati river areas, while millets predominated in the Saurashtra area. The Harappans were the first to grow cotton: in fact, it became the premium export commodity. Mehrgarh, which ante-dated the Harappan Civilisation, takes cotton cultivation to the fifth millennium BCE. As we noticed, granaries have been discovered in Mohenjo-daro, Harappa and Dholavira, indicating a production capacity that was surplus.

Some more on what the Harappans grew: *Ragi, jowar,* melons, peas, dates, bananas, grapes. They also grew jasmine and *pārijāta.*

AGRICULTURE: PLOUGH

This particular terracotta model of plough (Fig. 9.3) was found at Banawali in Haryana. It is dated around 2500 BCE. More pieces were found at other sites belonging to the same period. Similar ploughshares are still used in Haryana and Rajasthan.

The Harappans used the same type in Mohenjo-daro and Harappa, though, the samples available were broken and did not give a complete picture.

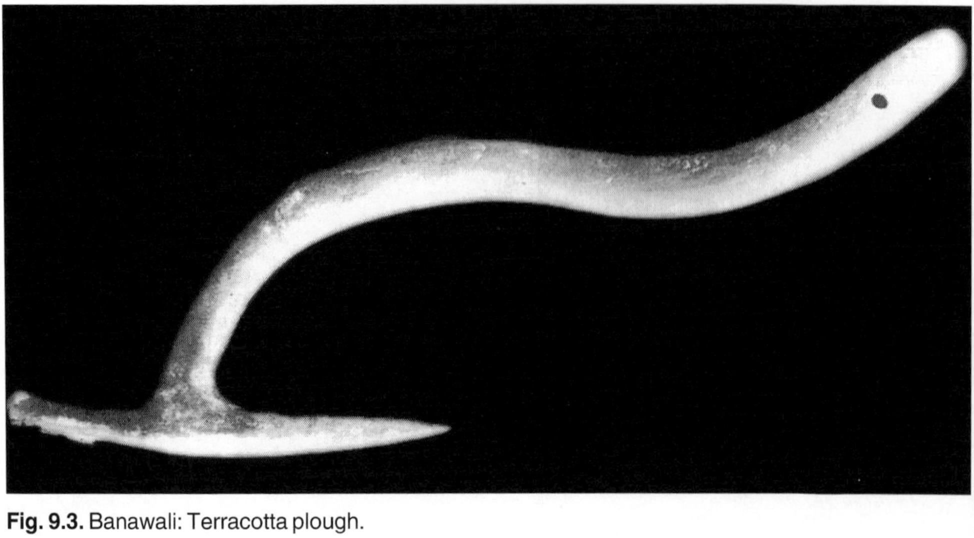

Fig. 9.3. Banawali: Terracotta plough.

AGRICULTURE: WELLS/RESERVOIRS

Water supply for agriculture was obtained from reservoirs and wells. There is evidence of canals, by damming up the rivulets. A well excavated at Dholavira is shown at Fig. 9.4. The marks of rope can also be seen. It can well be surmised that the water was lifted from the well and evacuated on the slab meant for the purpose, perhaps in exactly the manner in which we see it being done with bullocks in villages.

Earlier, while dealing with Dholavira, we drew attention to large-sized, rock-cut reservoirs which fully met the needs of the people.

Fig. 9.4. Well at Dholavira, showing abrasion marks left on the horizontal slab by the ropes moving up and down.

Fig. 9.5. Nausharo: Use of vermilion. (Pl. 17)

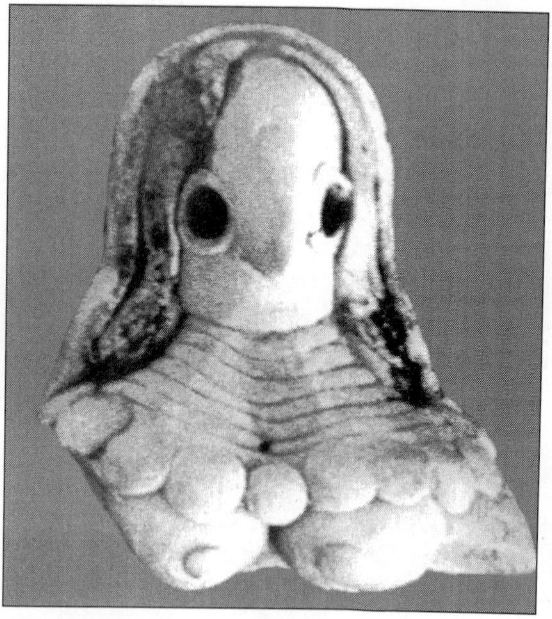

Fig. 9.6. Nausharo: Use of vermilion. (Pl. 18)

TRADITION: SINDŪRA

Fig. 9.5 and 9.6 show two of the several terracotta figurines found in an excavation in Nausharo in Pakistan by a French excavator, Jean-Francois Jarrige. These are dated to about 2800-2600 BCE. In these figurines, the body has usual terracotta colour and the ornaments are painted in yellow so as to indicate that these were made in gold. The lady's hair is parted, is black in colour and in the centre of the parting there is a red paint. This clearly represents the application of *sindūra* (vermilion) — a remarkable statement of continuity of our culture.

Use of *sindūra* today by married ladies needs no introduction.

TRADITION: YOGA

Yoga is India's gift to the world. Patanjali, the expert on Yoga school of philosophy in the second century BCE, in his treatise *Yogasūtra* delineates eight steps which lead to spiritual upliftment. Called *aṣṭaṅga yoga*, the steps are *yama, niyama, āsana, prānayāma, pratyāhara, dhāranā, dhyāna and samādhi.*

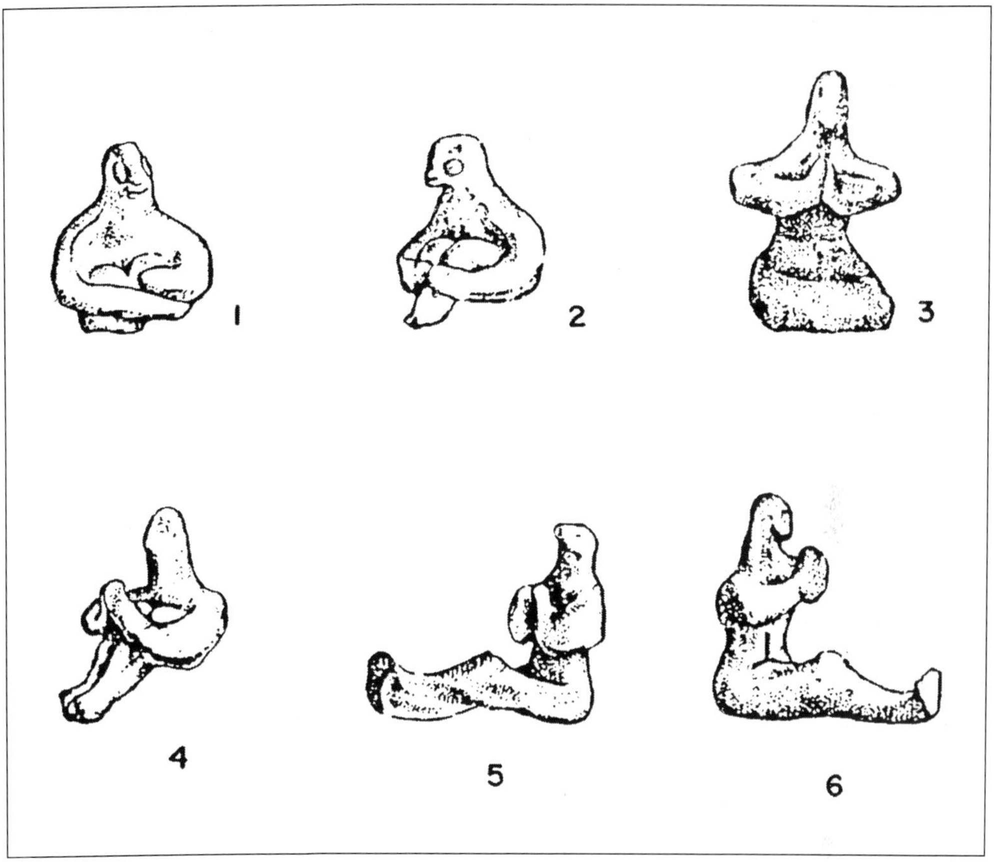

Fig. 9.7. Harappan terracotta figurines in yogic *āsanas.*

The present-day Yoga which is most common in the USA and Europe but lesser in other continents, has nothing to do with spiritual upliftment. It has more to do with physical *āsanas* and breathing exercises to keep one's body and mind in good health.

Terracotta human figures in yogic *āsana* (poses) have been discovered at Harappa and Mohenjo-daro, dating back to circa 2500 BCE (Fig. 9.7). Also, a limestone statuette discovered at Mohenjo-daro, seen earlier, showed a priest with his eyes half-open in meditation, that is, in *dhyāna-mudrā* or even in *samādhi.*

It is evident that yoga was in vogue as much as 2,000 years before Patanjali penned it down. As will be appreciated, it is not

Fig. 9.8. Mohenjo-daro: Swastika motif engraved on a seal. (Pl. 19)

Fig. 9.9. Entrance to a Hindu house with Swastika symbol. (Pl. 20)

possible to find tangible evidence of *yama, niyama* since these are a state of mind.

TRADITION: SWASTIKA

The symbol dates back to the Harappan times, the seal shown in Fig. 9.8 having been discovered at Mohenjo-daro.

Amongst the most prominent Hindu symbols is the *swastika*. It is derived from Sanskrit words *su* meaning 'good' or 'auspicious' and *asti* meaning 'to be', thereby literally meaning 'to be good'. It is a sacred symbol that is believed to bring good luck and fortune and is considered to imply success in future. It means 'promising' or of 'good omen'. It may be noticed on newly bought cars, or at the entrance of houses (Fig. 9.9), or at marriages, or while installing a new machinery.

TRADITION: NAMASTE

A greeting that needs no introduction even to the West. *Namaste* is actually *namah* meaning 'I bow' and *te* meaning 'to you'. The 'you' is actually not you by name or being, it is bowing to the 'god within you'.

The terracotta figure at Fig. 9.10 was discovered at Harappa and dates back to the third millennium BCE.

Fig. 9.10. Harappa: A terracotta figurine greeting with 'namaste'. (Pl. 21)

Fig. 9.11. Bronze statuette of a dancing girl from Mohenjo-daro. (Pl. 5)

Fig. 9.12. Lady wearing spiralled bangles. (Pl. 22)

LADIES' MAKE-UP: BANGLES

This bronze statuette of a girl was found at Mohenjo-daro (Fig. 9.11). It is dated to Mature Harappan period which is roughly 2500 BCE. Notice the necklace and the series of bangles on the left arm. The wearing of multiple bangles on the arms is still a custom amongst the rural women in Rajasthan, Haryana and Gujarat (Fig. 9.12). These are the areas in India where the Harappan Civilisation flourished five millennia back.

We have seen a set of spiralled bangles of silver found at Kunal, Haryana, dating back to Early Harappan, almost a thousand years before this girl was sculpted with bangles in her arm.

LADIES' MAKE-UP: CONICAL ORNAMENT ON THE HEAD

The conical ornament shown in Fig. 9.13 is called *chauk*. Made of gold, it was discovered at Mohenjo-daro and is datable to the

Mature Harappan times. Pandit Madho Swarup Vats, in his report on Harappa, states that the *chauk* is regarded as an important ornament to be given in marriage to one's daughter-in-law. It is usually worn at weddings and important religious ceremonies.

Fig. 9.14 shows a lady whose head is covered with a piece of clothing, under which there is a *chauk*. The practice of wearing a *chauk* is still prevalent in northern India.

Fig. 9.13. Gold cone from Mohenjo-daro. (Pl. 23)

Fig. 9.14. Conical ornament and bangles. (Pl. 24)

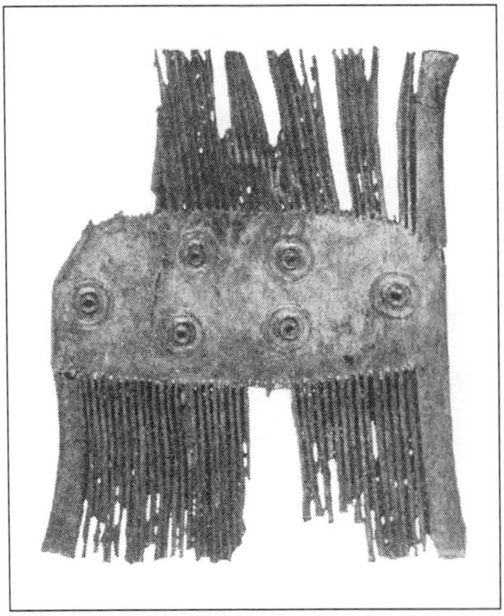

Fig. 9.15. Ivory comb from Mohenjo-daro.

LADIES' MAKE-UP: IVORY COMB

The ivory comb with teeth on both sides (Fig. 9.15) was discovered at Mohenjo-daro and dates back to Mature Harappan stage, around 2500 BCE. Notice that the teeth are thick on one side but somewhat finer on the other. Wooden combs, similar in shape, are still found in villages in northern India and are called *kakai*. A more modern version of the same, made of plastic, is also available in some markets.

LADIES' MAKE-UP: THREE-IN-ONE

This three-in-one personal toiletry item (Fig. 9.16) was discovered at Harappa. It is made of copper. Of the three pieces, the one with a pointed end is used as a tooth-pick. The one with a small cup is

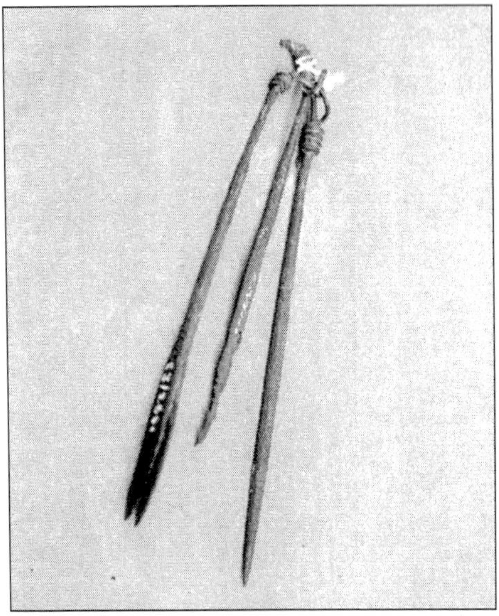

Fig. 9.16. A three-in-one toiletry item in copper from Harappa. (Pl. 25)

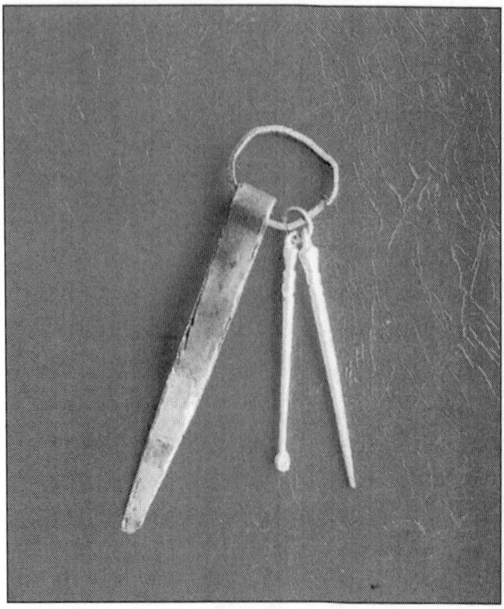

Fig. 9.17. A modern three-in-one toiletry item, copper. (Pl. 26)

used for taking out wax from the ears and the third one is, of course, the tweezers.

Beside it is placed a modern three-in-one version (Fig. 9.17), generally used by village folks. It was purchased in a market in Aligarh.

LADIES' MAKE-UP: BEADS

The area around Khambat in Gujarat specialises in making beads of semi-precious stones. The raw material is brought in the form of nodules, say of, agate and carnelian. These nodules are heated in a pot placed in an earthen furnace. These are then broken into required size and then shaped by flaking (Fig. 9.18). They are smoothened by rolling them in a drum filled with sand. Thereafter a hole is bored through the bead by a bronze drill. Heating them once again gives the bead the required finish.

Bead-making was a flourishing industry in Lothal and Chanhu-daro in the third millennium BCE. In Lothal, two jars were discovered in a courtyard, one containing 582 beads of carnelian while the other had 212 beads of carnelian, shell and steatite.

Fig. 9.18. A stage in bead-making process. (Pl. 27)

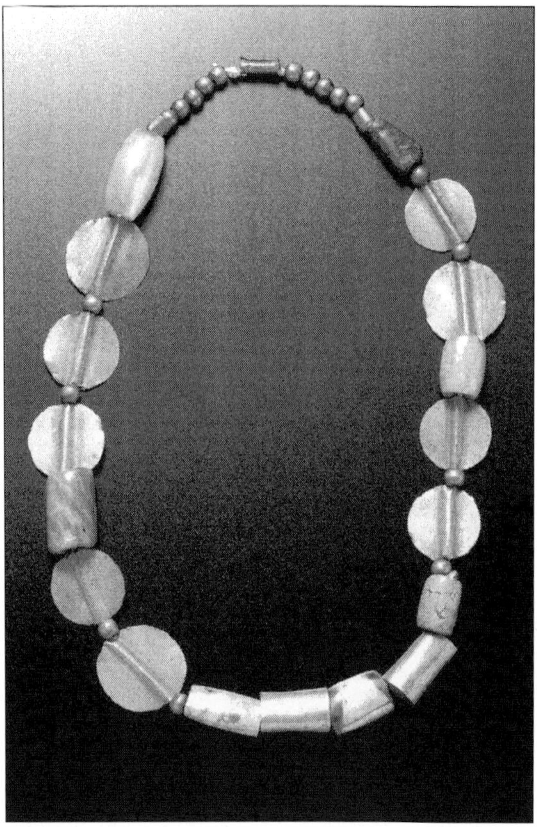

Fig. 9.19. Mohenjo-daro: Gold disc-beads. (Pl. 9)

Fig. 9.20. Mohenjo-daro: Gold necklace. (Pl. 10)

Along with the courtyard, more beads were found all over the connecting rooms. A bronze drill-bit used to drill holes and a kiln were also found. That the beads were also exported to contemporary Mesopotamia, Iran and central Asia was confirmed when beads were discovered in those areas.

The exports continued through the ages as can be seen from accounts of Hieun-Tsang (7th century CE). He refers to bead export to Egypt in west to countries in the east.

Some pictures are reproduced even at the cost of repetition in order to show how the ladies 5000 years ago liked to wear their ornaments.

Fig. 9.21. Gold beads from Dholavira. (Pl. 11)

Fig. 9.22. Gold disc-beads from Lothal. (Pl. 29)

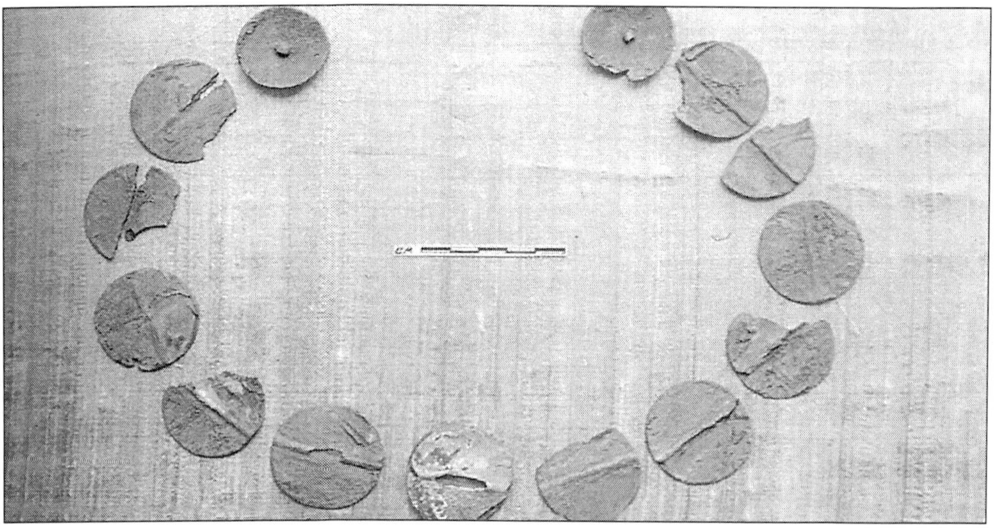

Fig. 9.23. Silver discular beads from Kunal for a necklace. (Pl. 30)

LADIES' MAKE-UP: NECKLACES

Fig. 9.23 shows beads in silver, from the Early Harappan levels of Kunal in Haryana, dating back to circa 3000-2800 BCE. Fig. 9.24 shows a necklace of similar beads in gold dating to Mature Harappan stage. It was discovered at Lothal in Gujarat. The beads are disc-like in shape, flattened and have perforations at diametrically opposite ends to allow the string to pass.

One can judge by their colours that they are of silver and gold respectively.

Even today, we can hope to purchase necklaces of similar beads at malls in Delhi or Dilli Haat or even in some villages in Rajasthan.

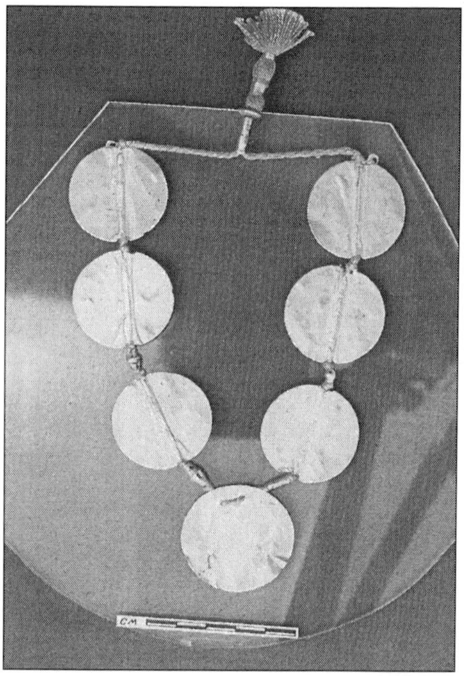

Fig. 9.24. Gold discular beads from Lothal for a necklace. (Pl. 8)

Fig. 9.25. Kalibangan: Śiva *liṅga*-cum-*yoni.*

Fig. 9.26. Śiva *liṅga*-cum-*yoni* in a modern temple. (Pl. 31)

RELIGION: *ŚIVA-LIṄGA*-CUM-*YONI*

Symbolic representation of Lord Śiva in temples has always been in the form of *liṅga*-cum-*yoni.* Excavations at Mohenjo-daro revealed stone objects in the form of *liṅga* and *yoni* indicating that the deity was worshipped then. This was dated to the third millennium BCE.

A more comprehensive example that leaves no doubt in anyone's mind that Śiva's symbol *liṅga*-cum-*yoni* was indeed worshipped during that period was discovered at Kalibangan, and is placed at Fig. 9.25.

RELIGION: ANIMAL SACRIFICE

Religion and rituals go together. To please a deity for a personal favour has long been a practice. How long? Fig. 9.27 shows the details of a seal discovered at Harappa. It depicts a Śiva-like figure in yogic posture with a three pronged headgear. In the centre is a man with a buffalo on the left. The man is pressing the buffalo's head with his leg, holding its horn with his left hand and in his right hand is a spear piercing the buffalo's

Fig. 9.27. A terracotta tablet from Harappa showing animal-sacrifice. (Pl. 12)

back, signifying the sacrifice to the lord. The practice is very much prevalent today in Himachal. Goat sacrifice is also well known.

As stated earlier, at Kalibangan a sacrificial pit was discovered containing bovine bones and antlers.

The seals leave no doubt that Lord Śiva occupied a very prominent place in the religious practices of the Harappans.

Fig. 9.28. Mohenjo-daro: *Kamaṇḍalu.*

RELIGION: *KAMAṆḌALU*

This *'Kamaṇḍalu'* which the *sādhūs* have been seen to carry (see them in the *Kumbh mela* in abundance) was found at Mohenjo-daro. It belonged to the Mature Harappan stage.

AT HOME: *TANDŪRS/CHULHĀ/ CHAKLĀ/BELAN*

Fig. 9.29 shows four *'tandurs'* excavated at Kalibangan, Rajasthan, dating back to 4,700 years.

Fig. 9.29. Clay *tandurs* in Kalibangan.

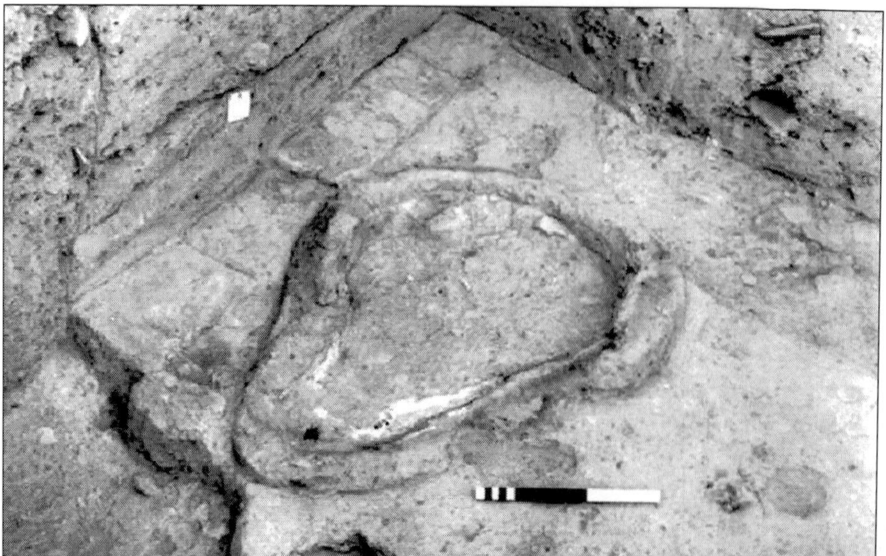

Fig. 9.30. *Chulhā*: Cooking hearth in Kalibangan.

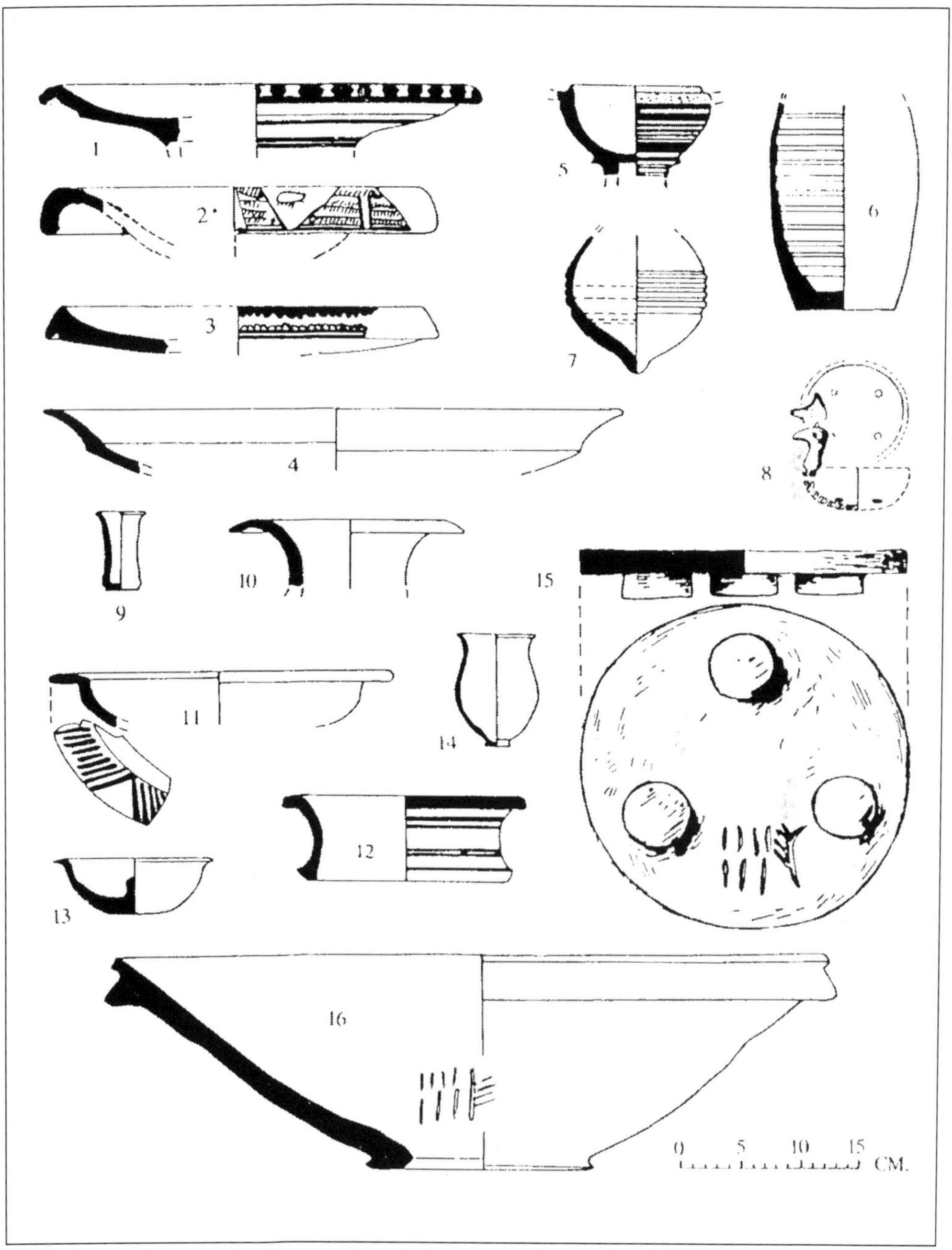

Fig. 9.31. *Chakla* (No. 15), Late Harappan at Alamgirpur.

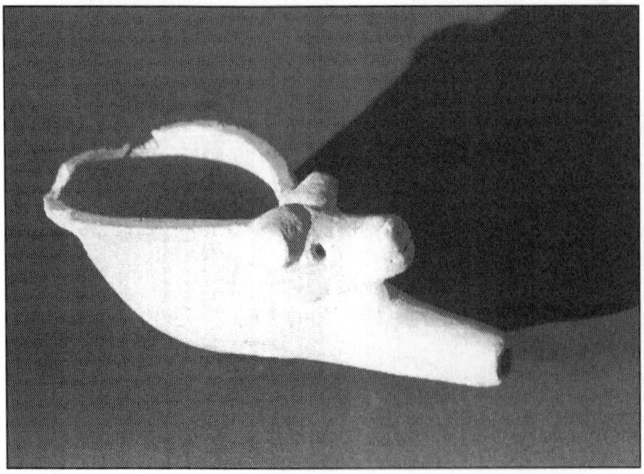

Fig. 9.32. A terracotta feeding cup from Kalibangan. (Pl. 32)

All that we have done since is to improve upon its heat efficiency by modifying its design!

U-Shaped cooking *chulhā*, which is a normal feature in villages even now, was also found in Kalibangan (Fig. 9.30).

Also see the *chaklā* at No. 15 in Fig. 9.31. It was found at Alamgirpur in a Late Harappan context. It was used for rolling the bread. No change has since taken place except that its legs have been shortened!

AT HOME: FEEDING CUPS

The Harappans used feeding cups for giving milk to the children. The terracotta specimen (Fig. 9.32) found at Kalibangan has an oval opening with a long spout. It also shows the face of a cow above the spout. Similar spouts, often in metal, are in use even today.

Fig. 9.33. *Takhtīs* from Mohenjo-daro.

AT HOME: *TAKHTĪ*

At Mohenjo-daro were discovered certain flat, rectangular terracotta objects which resemble in shape what are known as *takhtīs*. The two specimens illustrated in Fig.9.33 were found by Mackay who in fact described them as 'writing tablets'. Though made of terracotta and small in size (even the complete one measuring only 18 x 8 cm), these nonetheless have the typical small, rectangular extension at one end. This part has a hole, which in the case of actual wooden *takhtīs* these days is used for inserting a thread with which the tablet is hung on a nail affixed to a wall, after it has been used.

Fig. 9.34. A 2nd century BCE terracotta plaque from Yamunanagar.

That *takhtīs* of this very shape were used even in the third-second century BCE is established by a terracotta plaque found at a site in Haryana (Fig. 9.34). Though broken, it shows nonetheless a child holding a *takhtī* with his left hand, while with the forefinger of his right hand he points out a Brāhmī alphabet written on the *takhtī.*

Discovery of *takhtīs* tells us that there must have been a process to impart education nearly five millennia ago. Whether that was

Fig. 9.35. Today's children writing on *takhtīs.*

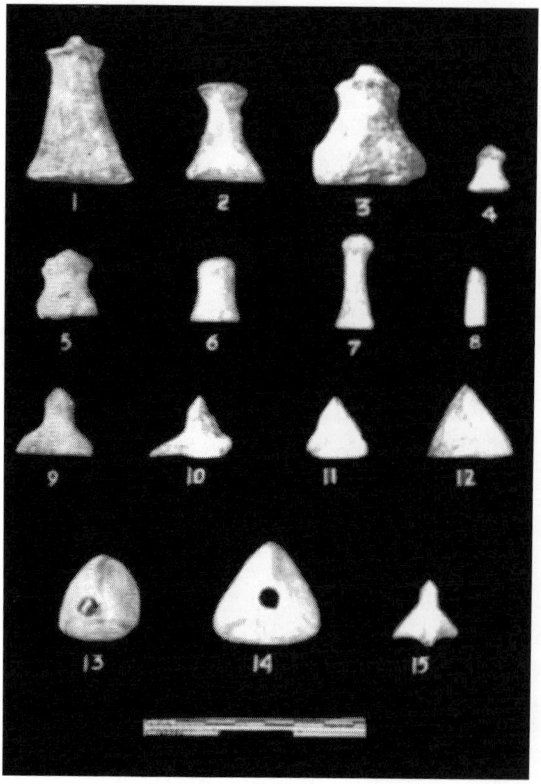

Fig. 9.36. Terracotta gamesmen from Lothal.

Fig. 9.37. Today's chess pieces.

done centrally through a medium of school or done at home is a moot point. Most probably, it had to be a school, or a central teaching point, where education was imparted for ensuring standardisation.

Though pen and paper have outdated *takhtīs* in primary schools in cities and towns, children in schools in some villages may still be seen using them (Fig. 9.35) Please note that the basic shape remains unchanged from the 3rd millennium BCE down to this day!

GAMES: CHESS

It is interesting to note that the game of chess goes back to the Harappan times. Fig. 9.36 shows gamesmen discovered at Lothal, in Gujarat. Fig. 9.37 shows how these were set on the chess-board.

GAMES: DICE

Cubical dice with 1-6 blind holes on its sides are used in games today. It is surprising that exactly the same type of dice were used as far back as 2500 BCE. Fig. 9.38 displays two such specimens from Mohenjo-daro, while Fig. 9.39 shows a modern example.

Fig. 9.38. Cubical dice in terracotta from Mohenjo-daro.

Fig. 9.39. A modern dice.

GAMES: PIṬṬU

Terracotta discs used in the game called *Piṭṭu* were discovered by Keyoner at Harappa (Fig. 9.40). Similar discs were found in Rakhigarhi excavations, piled up in a stack (Fig. 9.41).

Fig. 9.42 shows children at Harappa playing *Piṭṭu*, unaware of the fact that the same game was played in the same area 4500 years ago!

Fig. 9.40. Pottery discs from Harappa.

Fig. 9.41. Pottery discs from Rakhigarhi.

Fig. 9.42. Children playing *piṭṭu* at Harappa.

PETS: COLLARED DOG

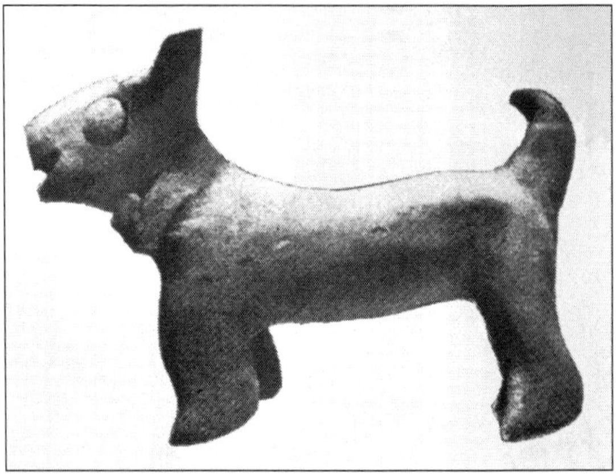

Fig. 9.43. Collared dog from Mohenjo-daro.

Don't think that we have the sole right to keep dogs as pets, put collar and leash around their necks and take them out on a morning walk. The accompanying photograph (Fig. 9.43) shows a terracotta dog around whose neck a collar has been tied. It comes from Mohenjo-daro and is datable to circa 2500 BCE. Is it possible that the Mohenjo-darians may have foreseen that the pets may have a collar but the stray could be left alone!

PETS: BIRD IN A CAGE

The keeping of pets by the Harappans was not confined to dogs. Here is an example (Fig. 9.44) which shows that birds were tamed and kept in a cage. This terracotta model comes from Harappa and is ascribable to the middle of the 3rd millennium BCE.

Side by side (Fig. 9.45) may also be seen a pretty little girl keeping watch over a cage with a partridge inside it. Aren't the

Fig. 9.44. A terracotta cage with birds, from Harappa. (Pl. 33)

Fig. 9.45. A modern cage. (Pl. 34)

past and present but facets of the same human attitude towards the avian world?

FABLES: THIRSTY CROW

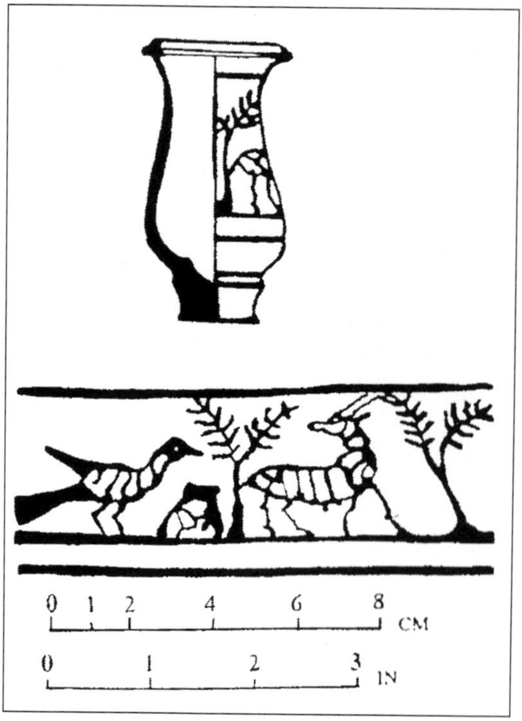

Fig. 9.46. A vase from Lothal, depicting the story of 'The Thirsty Crow'.

I don't know if your grandmother used to narrate tales to put you to bed. Anyway, my grandmother did. And today, after sixty years, I am surprised to find that some of these tales go back to the Harappan times – 4,500 years ago! I can't vouchsafe if the Harappan grandmothers also used to narrate these stories to their grandchildren, but I would love to imagine that they did.

The evidence of the Harappan fables comes from paintings on Harappan pottery. To be more precise, from Lothal, the well known Harappan settlement in Gujarat.

Fig. 9.46 shows a kiln-fired red ware vase on the exterior of which there is a scene painted in black colour. The details are given in the panel below the pot. Beginning from the left, one sees a crow, a pitcher, a tree, a deer and again a tree.

The outstretched right leg of the deer indicates that the animal is about to go away. However, his neck is turned backwards and he seems to be looking at the crow with amazement. The crow, in turn seems to be quite comfortable having just taken his beak out of the pitcher. The roundish objects in the pitcher are perhaps pebbles. The story would thus appear to be as follows:

There was a deer that was very thirsty. He came across a pitcher with some water in it. But the water-level was low and he could not insert his mouth in the pitcher because of his long horns.

Disappointed, he was about leave the place. Just then a crow appeared on the scene. He too was thirsty. Finding the water-level in the pitcher rather low, he too could not approach it. However, it occurred to him that if he dropped some pebbles in the pitcher the level of the water would rise and he would be able to drink it. He did the needful and drank water to his fill.

Moral: Think and you will find a solution

FABLES: CUNNING FOX

Yet another fable. In Fig. 9.47 may be seen two birds sitting on the branches of a tree, each holding a fish in the beak. The lower right part of the painting is damaged. Still a small hatched object may be seen. In the bottom left there is an animal which from its tail appears to be a fox. The story runs as follows. The cunning fox, wanting the feed himself, devises a plan to take it away from the birds. The fox tells the birds that they have a very sweet voice and requests them to sing for him. Flattered, the birds open their mouth to sing and as they do so, the fish falls off their beak and the fox runs away with the same.

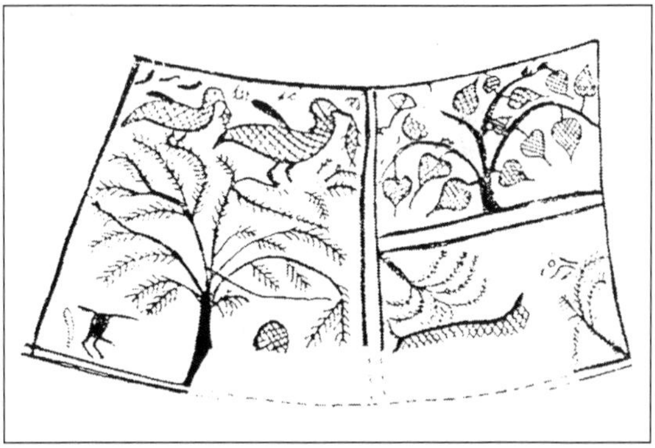

Fig. 9.47. Cunning Fox: Painting from Lothal.

Moral of the story: Don't give in to flattery.

The vase was discovered at Lothal and is 4500 years old.

SECTION 2

Allied Debates and Discussions

The Decline of Harappan Civilisation and Invalidity of 'Aryan Invasion' Theory 10

In this chapter, I intend discussing some probabilities on what caused the decline of Harappan Civilisation. I intend starting with Sir Mortimer Wheeler's Aryan invasion theory first.

The theory that the advent of Aryans in India took place in or around 1500 BCE was expounded in the 19th century by the then British rulers of India and their companion linguists in Europe. This has been discussed in a little more detail in the later chapters.

While excavating Harappa in 1946 (the excavations at Harappa had been a near continuous process), Sir Mortimer Wheeler, the then Director General of Archaeological Survey of India, unearthed a fortification wall which obviously was not in a perfect shape after 4500 years. Now since the *Ṛigveda* refers to Indra as '*puraṁdara*', meaning the destroyer of forts, he found a perfect 'reason' to support the already propounded advent of Aryans into India as the 'invasion' of Aryans into India. He announced that there was an Aryan Invasion (Indra being taken as signifying the Aryans) that destroyed the Harappan Civilisation. To force his claim, he described some skeletal remains found at Mohenjo-daro, as an evidence of the 'massacre'.

Also note that the entry into India of Aryans, as told to us by the British rulers in the 19th century, was dated to around

1500 BCE. Almost 150 years later, in 1946, Wheeler converted the entry into 'invasion'. We also know that the Harappan Civilisation started declining after the Mature phase around 2100-1900 BCE. Thus, if the decline was due to 'invasion' by the Aryans, how do these theorists explain the gap of about five centuries between the decline of Harappan Civilization and the supposed date of arrival of the Aryans?

Now, if there was an invasion as stated by Wheeler, the skeletal remains referred to by him would have been found at the uppermost level. This was not so. They came from various stratigraphic levels. There was no evidence of warfare, there were no injuries to the skeletons and in a few that bore cut-marks, their injuries had been healed (healing would not have taken place if death resulted from a war injury). Further, there were no weapons found at the level, there was no evidence of invaders in form of foreigners' remains (there is a definite 'no' from the biological evidence), or their weapons, no sign of their material culture having taken over the Harappan Civilisation.

Wheeler did not care to corroborate his statement with findings at Harappa which showed no evidence of any massacre. In fact, **no Harappan site, either in the Indus valley or the Sarasvati valley, shows any evidence of an invasion.**

Since then, many scholars have debunked this theory. Prof George F. Dales of University of California, Berkeley, Lord Colin Renfrew, Prof B.B. Lal, Michel Danino, J.M. Kenoyer, David Frawely and many others have written papers and made a reference in their books calling it a 'mythical massacre', 'An Invasion that Never Was', 'The Myth of Aryan Invasion' etc. Prof Hemphil, after a thorough analysis of skeletal data, holds that there was no biological discontinuity between 4500 BCE till after 800 BCE, thereby confirming that no foreign visitors (!) entered the subcontinent during that period.

Therefore since there was no invasion, that cause can be ruled out as the reason for the collapse of the Harappan Civilisation.

When 'invasion' was getting to be ruled out, there was a suggestion of 'migration' from a couple of Indian historians. Finding that there was no archaeological evidence to support invasion, Professor Romilla Thapar, a historian, hypothesised (1989-91:259-260): 'If invasion is discarded, then the mechanism of migration and occasional contact come into sharper focus. The migrations appear to have been of **pastoral cattle breeders** who are prominent in *Avestā* (a collection of sacred writings of Zoroastrian religion) and *Ṛigveda*'. Another historian from the same school of thought, Professor R.S. Sharma (1999:77) said: 'The pastoralists who moved to the Indian borderland came from Bactria Margiana Archaeological Complex (BMAC) which saw the **genesis of the culture of *Rigveda*'**. (BMAC Civilisation lay between Margiana in Turkmenistan in the west to Bactria in the east, which is north of Afghanistan).

If someone reads about the BMAC, he will realise that this Civilisation was not the product of pastoral cattle breeders. It was urban in nature, had palaces and temples, metal industries, highly advanced art form in limestone, chlorite and gold and high standard of seals. Please see Figs. 10.1 to 10.4 to get an idea of the high level of civilisation of BMAC. How can such a civilisation be led by ***pastoral cattle breeders***?

In any case, a few points need to be highlighted. No BMAC object ever ***crossed the Indus to its east***. This is evident from a close study of artifacts east of the Indus.

And if one adds to the western theory that Sanskrit was brought to India by the Aryans who, according to the migration theorists, were pastoral cattle breeders, then ***can you imagine the pastoral cattle breeders teaching that language to the inhabitants of the Harappan Civilisation spread over one million square kilometres***. And, of course, those ***pastoral cattle breeders writing about samrāṭ, rājā and rājan while composing the Ṛigveda!!***

Thus, the migration theory, too, is debunked.

Incidentally, about 60 years have elapsed before our NCERT books for junior classes have started saying that there may not have been an invasion. We don't know how many more years they will take to be certain about it. The academics all over the world barring a few are, however, certain that there was no invasion.

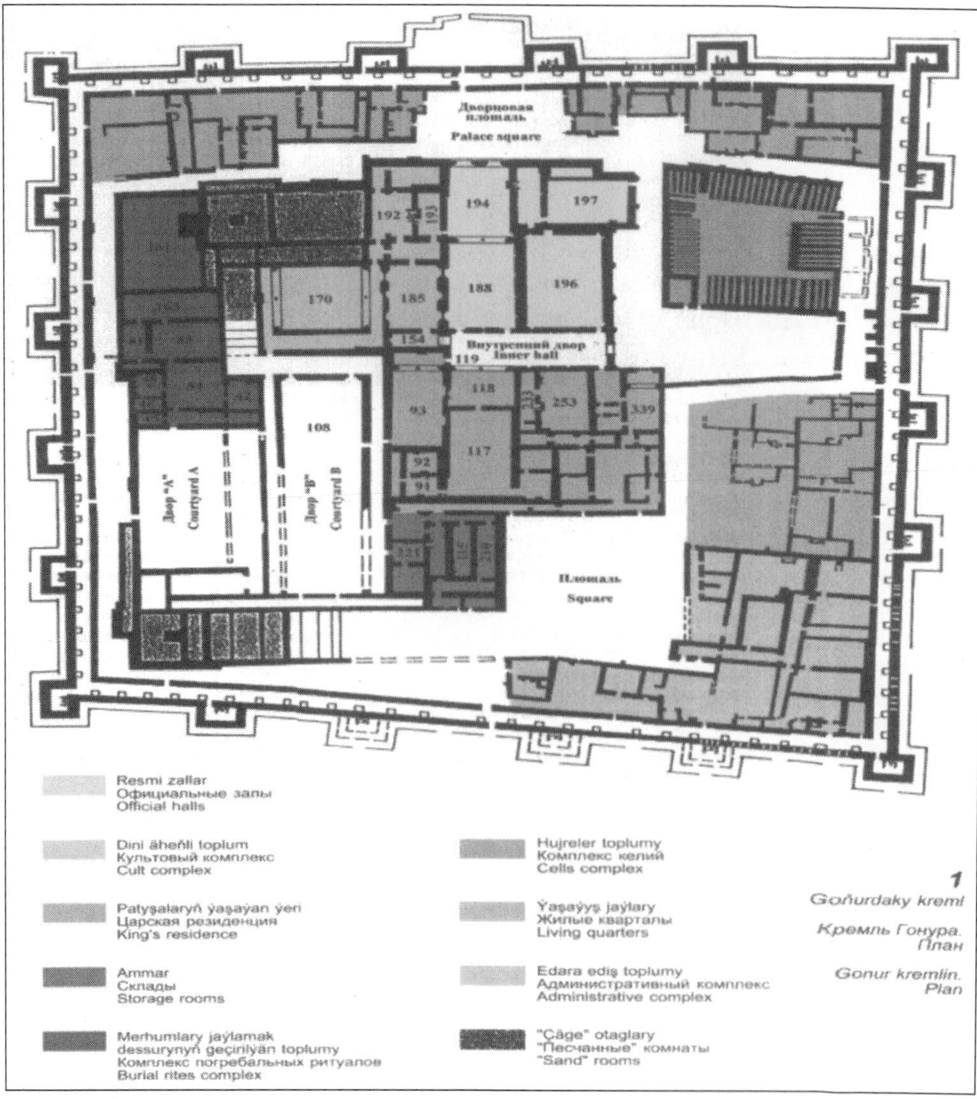

Fig. 10.1. Gonur, Margiana: Plan of Citadel. (Pl. 35)

Scholars have suggested many reasons for the decline of the Harappan Civilisation. One of the reasons suggested has been environmental factors. These include, variously, climate change, floods and drought. Any one of these factors could have seriously affected the agricultural output, and consequently, the survival

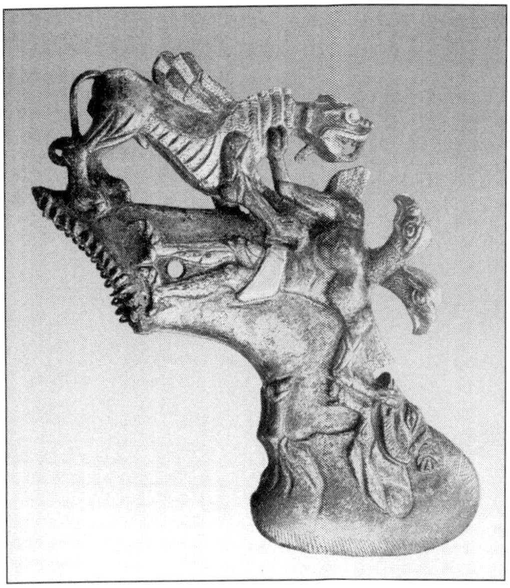

Fig. 10.2. Bactria: Silver ceremonial axe. (Pl. 36)

Fig. 10.3. Bactria: Composite stone figure. (Pl. 37)

of the cities. There is a theory about the flooding of Mohenjo-daro but that could not have wiped out the entire civilisation. Similarly, the drying up of Sarasvati due to tectonic shift caused by the Bata-Markanda divide could have caused drought in the areas relating the cities by the banks of Sarasvati/Ghaggar, but once again, the end of the civilisation could not be due to this alone.

Yet another reason could be this: This civilisation's grandstanding was due to its affluence and this accrued from agricultural surplus and internal and external trade. What may have happened is that climate change resulted in poor agricultural growth. The population began to leave cities and moved eastwards towards the upper Ganga-Yamuna doab. (There is evidence to that effect.) With the movement of population, two things happened. The 'urban' nature of cities started to turn 'rural'. A form of 'devolution' set in. The movement of population must have included the craftsmen, artisans, lapidaries, sailors, etc. That would have definitely affected the internal and external trade adversely. With trade marginalised, the agricultural growth

Fig. 10.4. Feline in semi-precious stone inlay. (Pl. 38)

reduced, it was only a question of time when the civilisation began to ebb.

That there is no single cause but that of *climate change over centuries* that caused the downfall is agreed to by experts. To study what caused the decline, they have studied the *post* Mature Harappan period of each Mature Harappan site, strata by strata to come to this conclusion. The civilisation had declined gradually but surely.

The population moved eastwards towards the upper Ganga-Yamuna doab sometime around the end of third millennium BCE and the beginning of second millennium BCE, say between 2100 BCE and 1900 BCE. The evidence is available, especially in three sites, viz. Alamgirpur, Hulas and Bargaon which lie in the region of north-western Uttar Pradesh. The combined evidence from these sites is in the form of pottery and antiquities which bear a strong semblance to the Late Harappan times.

With the information available as of date, it is largely a climate change that has been thought by the experts to be the cause of the decay of this civilisation. A few things are certain, though. Firstly, there was no invasion that wiped out this civilisation. Secondly, a gradual devolution took place resulting in the urban centres being downsized to rural ones by virtue of the fact that the population started leaving the cities.

Who Were the Inhabitants of the Harappan Civilisation? 11

WHAT THE TEXT BOOKS TOLD US

Our text books until the end of twentieth century and even in the first decade of twenty-first told us that around 1500 BCE, a group of people who spoke Sanskrit came pouring in from Central Asia. These people were called the 'Aryans' and entered the sub-continent from the north-west. Entering what is now Pakistan, they came across a highly developed civilisation along the river Indus. The text books also told us that the Indus valley was inhabited by the dark-skinned Dravidians. The Aryans, the people with fair skin, invaded the Indus Valley and sent Dravidians packing off to South India. We also learned that it was the Aryans, the invaders, who authored the *Ṛigveda*, supposedly by 12th century BCE, and it were they who spread Sanskrit throughout India. Most regrettably, it was not only in text books but also in major reference books and still holds a place on the net.

How this theory came about is discussed in the next chapter. But for the purpose of discussing/identifying the inhabitants of the Harappan Civilisation, the background that has been stated in the above paragraph would meet the requirement of this chapter.

If the Harappans were sent packing to South India, we would have found some sites that indicated that they had resettled there. Also, their new settlements in the south would have reflected the level of civilised society, their buildings, their culture and craftsmanship, et al. But there is no site in Andhra, Karnataka, Kerala or Tamil Nadu that bears any resemblance to the Harappan cities or their culture. Also, at that time what we had in South India was what is called the Southern Neolithic Culture, a culture that belonged to the end of the Stone Age. Certainly, the much superior Mature Harappan culture could not have regressed to Stone Age from Copper Age.

And since it has been accepted that there was no Aryan invasion or immigration, the statement that the so-called Harappan Dravidians were pushed to South India does not hold. The Dravidians, therefore, were not the original inhabitants of the Indus valley.

Who then?

THE *ṚIGVEDA* DESCRIBES ITS PEOPLE

As mentioned earlier, when the Aryan Invasion theory did not hold ground, there was a theory of immigration of **pastoral cattle breeders** from BMAC. Let us see if the *Ṛigveda* **describes its people as 'pastoral cattle breeders'**.

To be able to do that, there is a need to go into some verses of the *Ṛigveda* to know the type of people who inhabited the land. Far from describing them as nomads, these verses give us an insight into the rulers, the people and the level of advancement of the society.

Firstly on defence:

RV 7.15.14 *And, irresistible, be thou a mighty* ***metal fort*** *to us*
With hundred walls for man's defence.

RV 10.101.8 *...stitch ye [oh gods] the* ***coats of armour****, wide and many;*
Make metal forts, secure from all assailants.

On wealth, richness:

RV 9.33.6 *O Soma, from every side pour forth four seas filled with a thousand fold riches.*

RV 1.126.5 *Forty bay horses of ten cars' master before a thousand Lead the long procession.*
Feeling in joy Kaksivan's sons and Pajra's have grounded.the coursers decked with pearly trappings.

On the hierarchy of rulers the *samrāṭ* (emperor) and *rājan* (king) are mentioned. Another term, *rājakas* is not referred to in the following verses:

RV 6.27.8 *Two wagon teams, with damsels, twenty oxen, O Agni,* ***Abhyavartin Chayamana****,*
The liberal ***Sovran****, giveth me. This guerdon* (a reward) *of Prithu's seed is hard to win from others.*
Here Abhyavartin Chayamana is referred to as *Samrāṭ*.

RV 8.21.18 *Chitra is the King, and only kinglings are the rest who dwell beside Sarasvati.*
He like Parjanya with his rain, hath spread himself with thousand, yea, with myriad gifts.

An elaboration comes from *Śatapatha Brāhmaṇa*, verse V.1.1.13, which states:

By offering the Rājasūya he becomes Rāja and by the Vājapeya he becomes Samrāṭ, and the office of Rājan is lower than and that of Samrāṭ the higher. A Raja might indeed wish to become a Samrāṭ, for the office of Rājan is lower and of Samrāṭ the higher; but the Samrāṭ would not wish to become Rājā for the office of the Rājan is lower and that of Samrāṭ the higher.

(Note: The *Śatapatha Brāhmaṇa* is one of the nineteen *Brāhamaṇas* extant as of day. They are commentaries on the four Vedas. Two are associated with the *Ṛigveda*, six with *Yajurveda*, ten with *Sāmaveda* and one with *Atharvaveda*.)

On sea voyages:

RV 1.116.5 *O Aświns, you saved Bhujyu (from drowning) in a deep sea where there was nothing to hold on, by lifting him up in a boat* ***that had hundred oars*** *and sending him to his place. This was a brave act of yours.*

Would the above description of the society be that of pastoral cattle breeders who migrated from BMAC?

Secondly, BMAC as a civilisation was dated to 2000-1800 BCE whereas the description in the *Ṛigveda* conforms to the Mature Harappan period and which was at peak around 2500 BCE? **How can then one reconcile that a later civilisation gave birth to an earlier civilisation?**

To know who the real inhabitants were, we need to go into some time lines.

TIME LINES

We have seen the evolution of the Harappan Civilisation in earlier chapters: From Stage I in Bhirrana and Kunal, dated to around fifth to fourth millennium BCE, to Stage IV when the Harappan Civilisation was at Mature stage in the mid-third millennium BCE.

We have also seen that there were no invaders who destroyed this civilisation, or immigrants who occupied that land, and that anthropologically, there is no evidence of any outside race having entered India between 4000 BCE and 800 BCE.

Then where is the confusion? To understand the 'confusion', let us start when India was a colony of Britishers and we listened to their pronouncements as 'gospel truths'.

In late 19th century, Max Müller, a renowned German scholar, was tasked by Macaulay who had served in India as chairman of Education Board, to edit the 'Sacred Books of the East'. He dated the Vedas to 1200 BCE as the time when they were composed. It was an ad hoc date to which many of his contemporaries objected. In 1890, he climbed down from this dating and said:

> If now we ask how can we fix the date of these periods, it is quite clear that we cannot hope to fix a terminum a qua [sic].
>
> Whether the Vedic hymns were composed [in] 1000 or 1500 or 2000 or 3000 BC, no power on earth will ever determine.

Even though Max Müller agreed that 1200 BCE was not a correct assumption and it could have been as early as 3000 BCE, there was a sustained attempt by 'vested interests' (we will discuss these 'vested interests' later) to stick to this date.

When the Harappan Civilisation was discovered in early twentieth century and was dated to third millennium BCE, its obvious fallout was that this civilisation *pre-dated* the *Ṛigveda* and other Vedas.

Ergo, the civilisation could not be associated with Vedic people.

Twenty-five years or so later, in 1946, Sir Mortimer Wheeler declared that the Aryans invaded the sub-continent. Remember '*puraṁdara*', the destroyer of forts; that was the Aryan god Indra mentioned in the Vedas. The so-called Aryan invaders threw out the Dravidians to south of the Vindhyas, thus stating in no uncertain terms that the Dravidians were the authors of this civilisation who were pushed out due to invasion.

We have already said that there is no evidence of Aryan invasion or immigration from the central Asian region. Also, that there is no evidence of Harappan settlements in South India and that over there no site has been associated with that culture. In other words, the 'defeated' Harappans (read Dravidians from Wheeler's point of view) never existed. So who were the 'inhabitants'?

This 'approach' being a 'dead end', we will try a different approach through the *Ṛigveda* itself.

SPREAD OF THE ṚIGVEDIC PEOPLE

Ṛigveda's 10.75, verses 5 and 6, translated, are as follows:

> *O Ganga, Yamuna, Sarasvati, Sutudri (Sutlej), and Parusni (Ravi), O Marudvridha and Asikni (Chenab), O Arjikiya with Vitasta (Jhelum) and Sosuma (Sohan), please listen to and accept this hymn of mine. [5]*
>
> *O Sindhu (Indus), flowing, you first meet the Tristama (and then) the Susartu, the Rasa, and the Sweta (Swat), and thereafter the Kubha (Kabul), the Gomati (Gomal), the Krumu (Kurram) with Mehatnu; and finally you move on the same chariot with them (i.e. carry their waters with you). [6]*

Notice that verse 5 gives the true order of rivers from east, moving westwards. It also makes clear that the Sarasvati lay between the Yamuna in the east and Sutlej in the west. *Ṛigveda* 3.23.4 states that the Drisadvati and Apaya were its tributaries and *Ṛigveda* 7.95.2 mentions that the Sarasvati flowed all the way from mountains to the sea. (One scholar has mentioned that the Sarasvati was the river Helmand in Afghanistan: the flaw is that there is no Yamuna and Sutlej in Afghanistan and that the river Helmand in Afghanistan does no flow into the sea.)

So the *Ṛigveda* mentions that at the time when it was composed, the Sarasvati was a flowing river.

Panchaviṁśa Brāhmaṇa (XXXV.10.16) states that the river dried up in its time. But it does not tell us when? Fortunately, there are other disciplines that come to assist us in dating. And these are archaeological, hydrological, geological and radiocarbon methods of dating.

Geologists, when studying the history of the Sarasvati, have showed that the river originated from the Himalayan glaciers and flowed through the Shivaliks to descend on the plains. They further confirmed that the river had to change its course due to a tectonic movement in the Himalayas that created a wall 30 meters high blocking the flow of the river. The river perforce had to change its course in the south-easterly direction and merge with the Yamuna.

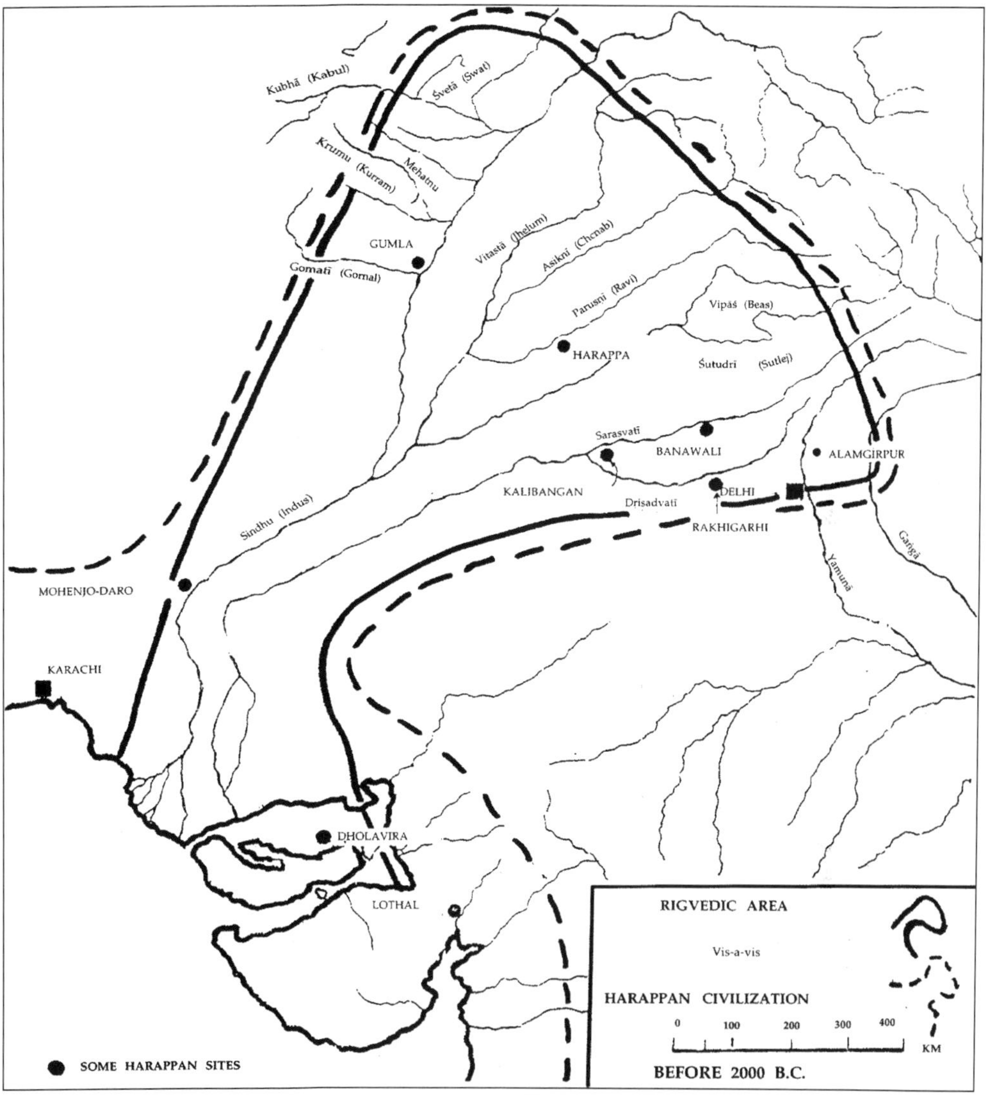

Fig. 11.1. Correlation between the Ṛigvedic area and the spread of Harappan Civilisation in the 3rd millennium BCE.

Next question: when did the tectonic movement take place that resulted in the drying up of the Sarasvati?

Since the Sarasvati was the lifeline of Kalibangan people, it was a natural corollary that the Kalibangan's demise took place at the time of its drying up. A team of hydrologists from India and Italy bored several holes in the bed of the now-dried river. In a paper published by the team leader to record the findings, it was stated that the site died due to the drying up of the river.

Once again, 'when'?

The radiocarbon dates puts the 'abandonment' to around 2000-1900 BCE.

The *Ṛigveda*, therefore, has to be earlier than 2000 BCE which means that we are looking into the third millennium BCE for its authors. It is also acknowledged by scholars that of the *Ṛigveda*'s ten *Mandalas,* numbers 3, 6 and 7 are the earliest. So the *Ṛigveda* could have been authored even earlier than the third millennium BCE, may be the fourth.

When the spread of the Indus Valley Civilization was discussed, it was stated that its western boundary was the river Indus. This was a known fact before Independence. Post-independence, the centre of this civilisation was found to be the Sarasvati valley, with its eastern edge going up to the upper Ganga –Yamuna doab. (No wonder, Indian and Western scholars have accepted the term Indus-Sarasvati Civilisation.)

Thus, the civilisation lay between the Ganga-Yamuna doab on the east and the Indus on the west.

How well it conforms to *Rigveda*'s verses 10.75, 5-6 above which state that the lay of the land was spread between Yamuna on the east and Indus on the west.

Thus the Harappan Civilisation and the *Ṛigveda* both belong to roughly 3000-2000 BCE.

It is, therefore, abundantly clear that the inhabitants of the Harappan Civilisation were the *Ṛigvedic* people themselves.

Genesis of the Aryan Invasion Theory

A Piece of 'Jigsaw' Push Fitted into the Mosaic of British Rule in India

12

It is my belief that Indian culture has deliberately been downsized for the sole purpose of British wanting to establish 'superior intellect' theory over the Indians. While it may be quite natural for the rulers, it was indeed demeaning to the country.

Let us begin by understanding why it was necessary to 'create' 'Indo-European Aryans' who then supposedly 'invaded' India to spread their culture and, of course, 'Sanskrit'. That they could have been 'pastoral cattle breeders' and had the capability to overrun a million and a half square kilometres of the Harappan Civilisation, as the textbooks and some Indian historians tell us, could that have been possible?

So here is my way of thinking.

Let us put a question to ourselves: Why did the British set foot in India. Why were we colonised? To know what attracted them, we must understand how India was perceived by the Europeans in mid-1700s and even later.

HOW INDIA WAS PERCEIVED IN THE 17TH-19TH CENTURIES

Voltaire (1694-1778), the French thinker, wrote:

> We have shown how much we surpass the Indians in courage and wickedness, and how inferior to them we are in wisdom. Our

> European nations have mutually destroyed themselves in this land where we only go in search of money, while the first Greeks travelled to the same land to instruct themselves.[1]

He, the great thinker, held this country in such awe that he said:

> I am convinced that everything has come down to us from the banks of Ganges, astronomy, astrology, metempsychosis, etc.[2]

William Macintosh (1778-1825), of Georgia, US, who was a native American chief, wrote:

> All history points to India as the mother of science and art. This country was anciently so renowned for knowledge and wisdom that the philosophers of Greece did not disdain to travel thither for their improvement.[3]

Pierre Sonnerat, a French naturalist, had said:

> India, in her splendour, gave religions and laws to all other peoples; Egypt and Greece owed to her both their fables and their wisdom.[4]

Sir William Jones, the founder of Asiatic Society of Calcutta, said the following of Sanskrit:

> [finds it to be] of wonderful structure, more perfect than the Greek, more copious than the Latin, and more exquisitely refined than the either.

The attraction for India was such that historian, Thomas R. Trautmann, puts across the sentiments of those looking towards this country as:

> ...the study of Sanskrit and Indian antiquities would bring a second renaissance to the West, as the study of Greek learning had been the foundation of the first renaissance.[5]

Friedrich Schlegel (1772-1829), who was a German poet, philosopher and an Indologist, said:

> Everything without exception is of Indian origin. Whether directly or indirectly, all nations are originally nothing but Indian colonies... The original antiquity could, if we consented to deepen it, bring us more safely towards the divine[6]

Tune onto 21st century. David Frawely, in his book, *Hidden Horizons*, tells us that Economist Angus Maddison makes a point in *The World Economy; A Millennial Perspective* that the Indian Subcontinent had the largest share of world's GDP until the end of 16th century and that India was the richest country for over 75% of the world's counted calendar of history.

India, then, was the "goose that lay the golden eggs".

WORLD PERCEPTION AFTER THE BRITISH HAD COLONISED INDIA

Dadabhai Naoroji, in 1766, about a decade after Battle of Plassey, a battle in which the British established their supremacy and laid a firm foundation for furtherance of their objectives of ruling India wrote:

> We have the strongest sense of the deplorable state [of] corruption and rapacity of our servants... a scene of the most tyrannic and oppressive conduct that ever was known in any age or country. Such unfortunately was the beginning of the connection between Britain and India—based on greed and oppression. And to our great misfortune and destruction, the same has remained in subtle and ingenious forms and subterfuges up to the present day with ever increasing impoverishment[7]

Anquetil-Duperron (1731-1805), a first professional French scholar of Indian culture, said in 1778:

> Peaceful Indians.....did the rumour of your riches have to penetrate a clime in which artificial needs knew no bounds? Soon, new foreigners reached your shores; inconvenient guests, everything they touched belonged to them....; it was not enough that they should invade your commerce, make the price of foodstuffs and goods triple, alter their quality; your factories almost wiped out.....[8]

William Digby (1849-1904), a British author and journalist, said in 1901:

> Time was, not more than a century and a half ago, when Bengal was much more wealthy than was Britain[9]

Brooks Adams (1838-1918), an American historian, said:

> Very soon, after Plassey [in 1757], the Bengal plunder began to arrive in London, and the effect appears to have been instantaneous, for all the authorities agree that the industrial revolution began with the year 1760...Possibly since the world began no investment has yielded the profit reaped from the Indian plunder[10]

Voltaire said,

> No sooner than India began to be known to the West's barbarians than she was the object of their greed, and even more so when these barbarians became civilised and industrious, and created new needs for themselves...[11]

So the first reason was to rule over a rich land.

Having achieved that, the second objective was to **establish religious and racial superiority over those being ruled.** It is in this context that the **theories of Aryan invasion took birth**, a topic relevant to our book.

At the beginning, there was indeed an interest in learning the Indian scriptures. To that end knowledge of Sanskrit was necessary. Having learnt that, the scriptures were translated into English.

What began as a genuine interest in knowing the scriptures turned into a tool, over a period, to tell the world how inferior was Hinduism to Christianity. Thoughts of Max Müller, who never set foot in India but who has a road named after him in Lutyen's Delhi, said of the translated scriptures:

> .. the whole human race required a gradual education before, in the fullness of time, it could be admitted to the truths of Christianity. To him the religion of India through its very errors... may have but served to prepare for the way of Christ.[12]

> I do not claim for the ancient Indian literature any more than I should willingly concede to the fables and traditions and songs of savage nations[13]

Not only Max Müller, but also M. Monier-Williams, H.H. Wilson, R.T.H. Griffith and E.B. Cowell amongst others joined in to denigrate the scriptures, especially the Vedas.

The next step was to establish superiority through language.

In the sixteenth century, European travellers to India noticed that there existed a striking similarity between Sanskrit on one hand and Persian, Celtic, Gothic, Latin and Greek on the other. They believed that the vocabulary and grammar of Sanskrit was the basis for those European languages. How William Jones (1746-1794), the Anglo-Welsh philologist and founder of Asiatic Society of Calcutta, turned Sanskrit into a language having an external source by the name of **Indo-European** language is evident from his famous statement (Jones, 1788):

> The Sanscrit (sic) language, whatever be its antiquity, is of a wonderful structure; more perfect than the Greek, more copious than Latin, and more exquisitely refined than either, yet bearing to both of them a stronger affinity, both in roots of verb and the forms of grammar, than could possibly have been produced by accident; so strong indeed that no philologer could examine all three, without believing them to have sprung from some common source, which, perhaps no longer exists; there is a similar reason though not quite so forcible, for supposing that both Gothic and Celtic, though blended with a very different idiom, had the same origin with the Sanscrit; and the old Persian may be added to the same category.

The name given to the common group of languages was 'Proto-Indo-European' language.

That statement hijacked the Sanskrit language from India and added European dimension to it.

Two things happened. One, that the Europeans could not accept that Sanskrit was a language from India. It had to be an Indo-European language, and if so, **there had to be an Indo-European race which spoke that language.** (The Aryans were referred to as a *race* by James Cowles Prichard in 1843.) Where was this race, which country did they live in? Various countries offered ownership. (Germany did that in 19th century.) Central Asia was the chosen one and the accepted one at that time. To the west of it, the Aryans became European Aryans. European Aryans were, of course, Christians, so necessary to oppose anti-Semitism prevailing in Europe at that time. **To the east of it, they became Indo-Aryans. The *Ṛigveda* was seen as "rather Indo-European**

than Hindu, and representing the condition of Aryans before their final settlement in India".[14]

Secondly, remember the 'Arya' of the *Ṛigveda*. The war that was described in the *Ṛigveda* between the Aryas and the Dasyus was the war between the good and evil. With the English translation of the *Ṛigveda* in the 19th century, the Aryas had already been transformed into the Aryan race and the Dasyus were identified as the Dravidians. Scene was set for the myth to be perpetuated that it was the Aryan race from Central Asia which invaded and overran India, throwing the Dravidians, the then inhabitants of Indus valley in the north, to the south of the Vindhyas. That created the Aryan/ Dravidian divide and the divide between the north of so-called Aryans (the victors) and the south, the so-called victims, the Dravidians.

Summarily, their broad-based argument went something like this: Aryans were the masters of Sanskrit language. They were from Central Asia. Sanskrit is now the language of India for centuries. Who brought it to India, the Aryans, of course. And how did they do that? By invading, or by immigration, if not the former!

That was the genesis of Aryans entering India around 1500 BCE with the *Ṛigveda* being composed around 1200 BCE; and later, Wheeler provided the icing on the cake by introducing the 'Aryan invasion theory'.

Now it was easy for them to say that we, the Britishers, the original Aryans belonging to the European Aryan branch, and the direct descendants of the race that ruled India once, it was our second home-coming in the 18th century.

Nobody, none of the philologists, theorists, has explained how this entire country could grasp, understand, read and write the language in the absence any literature belonging to the Aryan age, barring the inscriptions on the seals. What happened to the native language of the land that is supposed to have been overrun? And which country that is supposed to be the homeland of Aryans has retained Sanskrit as its language other than India? Do the Europeans or the Central Asian countries that are the supposed domicile of Aryans still have Sanskrit as their language?

Nonetheless, they pursued their theory.

John Wilson, who was a missionary in 1850s remarked:

> What has taken place since the commencement of British rule in India is only a reunion, to a certain extent, of the members of the same great family, with the most enlightened and philanthropic nation in the world[15]

Max Müller, who also has a 'Bhavan' named after him apart from the road, mentioned:

> ...how the [English] descendants of the same [Aryan] race, to which the first conquerors and the masters of India belonged, return to accomplish the glorious work of Civilisation, which had been left unfinished by their Arian brethren.[16]

Superiority was complete. India's pride was down and out, India's scriptures were not theirs but belonged to the Aryans, and Vedic gods like Indra, Varuna were not Indians, roots of Hinduism did not originate in India, etc.

In his autobiography, Max Müller, well aware how the invasion theory had worked, wrote:

> Lord Derby, then Secretary of State for India, declared that the scholars who had discovered and proved the close relationship between Sanskrit and English, had rendered more valuable service to the [colonial] government of India than many a regiment.[17]

As it stands today, enough evidence exists and writings of scholars all over the world have shown the theory as having been debunked. In conclusion, I will reproduce two much respected personalities in our recent history, Sri Aurobindo and Swami Vivekanand.

Sri Aurobindo (1971:24) had this to say:

> The indications in the Veda on which this theory of a recent Aryan invasion is built are very scanty in quantity and uncertain in significance. There is actually no mention of such invasion.

Swami Vivekanand did not mince any words and had this to say (1970-73: Vol 5, 534-535):

> And what you European pundits say about Aryans swooping down from some foreign land and, snatching away the lands of

> the aborigines and settling down in India by exterminating them, is pure nonsense, foolish talk! In what Veda, in what Sukta do you find that the Aryans came to India from a foreign country? Where do you get the idea that they slaughtered the wild aborigines? What do you gain by talking such nonsense? Strange that our Indian scholars too, say amen to them; and all these monstrous lies are being taught to our boys!

Views of two foreign scholars are reproduced. Firstly, Colin Renfrew who wrote (1988:188 and 190):

> When Wheeler speaks of 'The Aryan Invasion of Land of Seven Rivers, the Punjab', he has no warranty at all, so far as I can see. If one checks the dozen references in the Rigveda to the seven rivers, there is nothing in any of them that to me implies an invasion....Despite Wheeler's comments, it is difficult to see what is particularly non-Aryan about the Indus valley.

Two eminent archaeologists from USA, Jim G. Shaffer and Diane Lichtenstein (1999), also disagree with the 'Invasion' theory:

> A few scholars have proposed that there is nothing in the 'literature' firmly placing the Indo-Aryans outside of South Asia, and now archaeological record is confirming this...As data accumulate to support cultural continuity in South Asian prehistoric and historic periods, a considerable restructuring of existing interpretive paradigms must take place. We reject most strongly the simplistic historical interpretations, which date back to eighteenth century, that continue to be imposed on south Asian cultural history. These still prevailing interpretations are significantly diminished by European ethnocentrism, colonialism, racism and anti-Semitism.

Regrettably, some Indians still live in a historical world constructed by some foreigners, and will continue to do so until someone one day who is responsible for Indian history decides to read research papers published since independence, see evidences of archaeology and associated disciplines and update his knowledge and update writing of our text books. Till then we are doomed to the foreign version in school text books and higher institutes of learning, the concerned authorities having allowed westerners to interpret Indian history and culture.

Aryan Invasion Theory (AIT) versus Out of India (OIT) Theory 13

In Chapter 11, we attempted to establish that the Ṛigvedic people were the authors of the Harappan Civilisation. In Chapter 12, we saw why and how the British rulers laid the foundation of the theory of Aryans' entry into India in 1500 BCE and later, the Indian historians modified the 'invasion' into 'immigration', none of which withstood the scientific scrutiny of archaeology, anthropology and related sciences.

It is also evident that no cognisance has been taken by the 'mainstream view' theorists of the excavations carried on the Indian side since Independence which have revealed that the Harappan Civilisation that was considered to be limited to Indus valley had in fact extended to the entire Sarasvati valley and Gujarat, thus manifesting the extent of the civilisation to about one and half million square kilometres.

Then with Aryan Invasion theory discredited, the home of Aryans still not found in Central Asia or in Balkans, or in Scandinavia or Europe even after three centuries of propounding that theory, how is it that we find evidences and references of Aryans in Turkey and Iran?

First, the evidence in Turkey.

Hugo Winckler (1863-1913) was a German archaeologist and historian. He excavated Bogazkoy in Turkey between 1906 and

1912. His excavations revealed thousands of clay tablets with inscriptions on them. His finds proved that the city was once a capital of a great empire.

Amongst his inscriptional finds was evidence about the presence of Aryans in that region in 14th century BCE. In certain tablets was inscribed a treaty between a Mitanni king named Matiwaza (Mitanni was an area between the old north Syria and south-east Anatolia, present north Syria and Asian Turkey to its west) and a Hittite king Suppiluliuma (Hittites were people from north central Anatolia). The treaty was dated 1380 BCE. As witness to this treaty, the kings invoked the **Vedic gods *Indra, Mitra, Nāsatya* and *Varuṇa*.**

The tablets other than the above reveal more than a hundred Sanskrit names. Some of these are *Biridasva* (=Vedic *Vridhasva*); *Uruditi* (no change from Sanskrit); *Artasumara*, another Vedic king (=Vedic *Ritasmara*) as well as *Matiwaza* (=Vedic *Mativaja*). Some of the tablets go back to 17th century BCE.

There are documents dealing with horse training which have Sanskrit numerals, artefacts and art, the latter dating back to 17th, perhaps as much as 20th century BCE, depicting peacock, a bird typical of India and, in fact, its national bird. It is not a bird of Central Asia or west Asia. We need to ask ourselves as to how did the bird get there?! The answer lies in the fact that someone had taken the bird in art form to that area.

Who?

The Aryans themselves.

T. Burrow (1909-1986) was an Indologist and the Boden Professor of Sanskrit at Oxford University from 1944 to 1976. He observed (1955): 'The Aryans appear in Mitanni from 1500 BCE as the ruling dynasty, which means that they must have entered the country as conquerors'.

The 'mainstream' theorists theorised that Aryans must have been *on way to India* prior to their entry into India in 1500 BCE. Their stand was also based on Max Müller's dating of the Vedas to 1200 BCE whereas the Bogazkoy inscription was dated to 14th century BCE. With Max Müller's dating off by over a millennium and a half, the arguments do not hold.

The second argument that they put forward was that this very region was the 'original home' of Aryans. This means that the local population was of Aryans. This was not so as stated by Burrow. Further, had it been so, the language of Sanskrit would have been the basic language in Syria and Turkey region.

Now that we now know that there was no Aryan movement into India, the obvious corollary that presents itself **is that the Aryans in Mitanni came from India. To drive home the point, let it be stated that there was no other country in the world except India where the Vedic gods mentioned above were being worshipped.** It were the Aryans from India who invoked these gods in the aforesaid treaty. The second unassailable fact is that having established that the *Ṛigveda* is a document of at least third millennium BCE and written in India, there is no chronological obstacle in the path to accept that fact that the Aryans were the carriers of the Vedic knowledge to the west.

There is also relationship between the Ṛigvedic people and the people of Iran. The *Āvestā* is the sacred book of Zoroastrians. Its language is close to that of the *Ṛigveda*. The most conspicuous difference is that the Ṛigvedic 's' becomes 'h' in the *Āvestā*. Evidence suggests that the *Āvestā* was composed in 14th-11th century BCE; another view is that is of 11th-8th century BCE. In any case, it is composed much later than the *Ṛigveda*.

The *Āvestā* refers to *Devas* and *Asuras*, however, their meanings get reversed. It also refers to *'Yoi Hapta Hendu'*, which is the *Satpta Sindhu* of the *Ṛigveda*. Such a mention of Ṛigvedic land of 'seven rivers' in the *Āvestā* could have been only by the people who had been once in the land of 'seven rivers'.

But the most telling evidence is from another Vedic text, *Baudhāyana Śrautasūtra*.

The English translation of text number 18.44, (a copy of the original text is placed as Fig. 13.1) runs as follows:

'Āyu migrated eastwards. His (progeny) are the Kuru-Pāñchalas and Kāśī-Videhas. This is Āyava migration.

Amāvasu migrated westwards. His (progeny) are the Gāndhari, Paraśu and Araṭṭa. This is Amāvasva migration'.

The sons of Aila Puraravas and Urvaśī, named Āyu and Amāvasu migrated respectively to east and west. Āyu, migrating

[१८ । ४४, ४५ ।]　　बौधायनश्रौतसूत्रम् ।　　३९७

अथ रहरागच्छेयुस्तदाग्नना स्यां । न त्वा नग्नं पश्येयमिति ।
सर्वमेवैतद्भगवति सुकरमिति होवाच । कथा त्वपि[१] जाया
पतिं नग्नं न पश्यतीत्यन्तर्वासं वसीया[२] इति होवाचानग्नो
भवेति[३] । तथा सहोवासान्तर्वासं वसानः । सा ह स्म जाता-
ञ्जातानेव पुत्रानपविध्यति । तान् ह राजोवाच पुत्रकामा ह
वै भगवति वयं मनुष्याः स्मो जाताञ्जातान् त्वमपविध्यसीति ।
सा होवाच पर्यवेतरा वयो भवन्ति क्षीणायुषो ऽन्ये । भूयः
प्रियं करवावहा इति । सायुं[४] चामावसुं च जनयां चकार ।
सा होवाचेमौ बिभृतेमौ[५] सर्वमायुरेष्यत इति । प्राङायुः
प्रवव्राज । तस्यैते कुरुपञ्चालाः[६] काशिविदेहा इत्येतदायवं
प्रव्राजं । प्रत्यङ्मावसुस्तस्यैते गान्धारय[७] स्पर्शवो ऽराट्टा
इत्येतदामावसवम्[८] । ॥ ४४ ॥

अथो हास्या एषा पूर्वचित्तिरप्सरा स्वसा बभूव । सा
हेर्ष्यां चक्रे ज्योग् वै मे स्वसा मनुष्येष्ववात्सीद्धन्तैनामच्छाया-

---

१ त्वपि L, त्वपि the other MSS.

२ वसीया L Be (sec. m.) वासीत्याग्य the other MSS.

३ भवति MSS. exc. L, which has वेन च वासनो भवतीति ।

४ प्रायुं Be (sec. m.).

५ बिभृते॰ Be L ; the other MSS. om. these words.

६ ॰पांचालाः L B.

७ The proper names given acc. to Be (sec. m.) ; the other MSS. गांधारा (or री) पयस्पर्शवोह्लारा (or त्य) मा (or वा) ।

८ इत्येतन्मावसुम् or इत्येतन्मामवसुम् or इत्येतन्मामावसम् MSS.

Fig. 13.1. Photocopy of relevant text in Sanskrit from *Baudhayāna Śrautasūtra.*

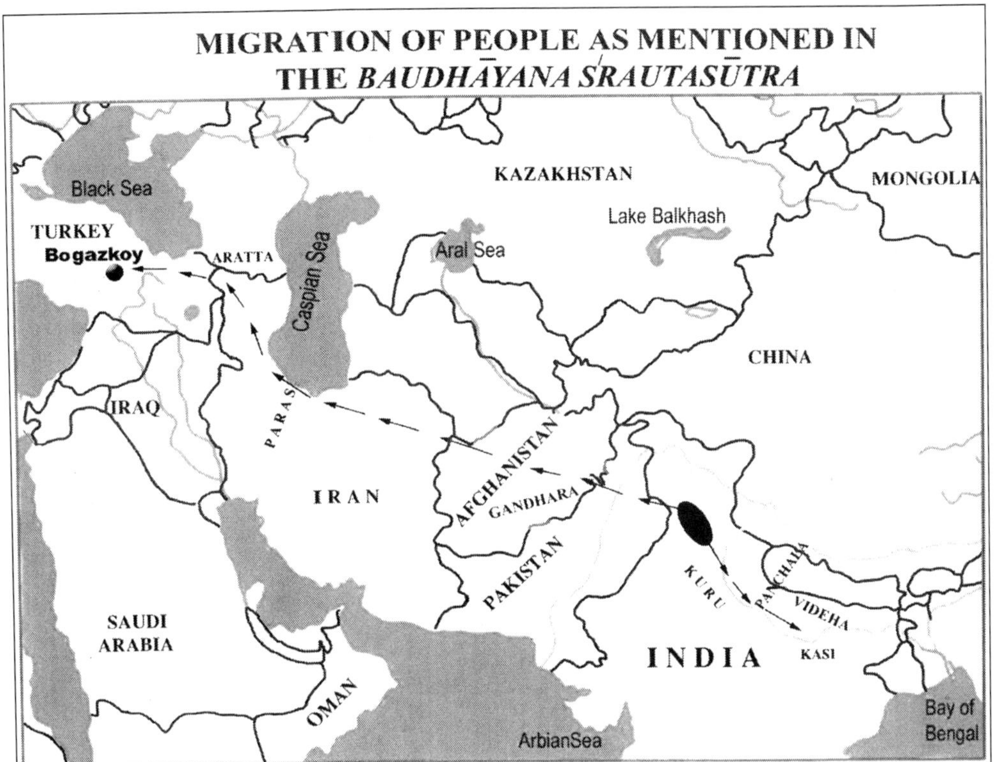

Fig. 13.2. Migration of people as mentioned in *Baudhayāna Śrautasūtra.* (Pl. 39)

eastwards, went to Kuru-Pāñchala and Kāśī-Videha. Amāvasu, migrating westwards, went to Gandhāra, Paraśu and Araṭṭa.

Identification of these places is not difficult. Kuru is present day eastern Haryana, Pāñchāla is western Uttar Pradesh, Kāśī is Varanasi, eastern Uttar Pradesh and Videha is western Bihar.

Gandhara is Kandahar in Afghanistan, Paraśu is Persia (Iran since 1935) and Araṭṭa is an area close to north of Iraq, also mentioned in a Sumerian epic.

So where were the two sons located before moving east and west? The bifurcation evidently took place from an area which was between the Kuru region on the east Gandhara region on the west. In other words, their habitation prior to bifurcation lay in the Panjab area. See Fig. 13.2.

14 In Conclusion

The partition of India gave impetus to archaeologists on the Indian side to carry forward the exploration and excavation of the sites that could have been connected to the Harappan Civilisation. Fully aware of the fact that any civilisation would flourish alongside a river, explorations followed by excavations were carried out along river-beds and mounds on the Indian side that lay east of the Indus. Sites that gave us major insights into the Harappan Civilisation are Kunal, Bhirrana, Banawali, Rakhigarhi and Kalibangan in the ancient Sarasvati basin and its tributaries. In Gujarat, contemporary sites are Lothal, Dholavira and Surkotada. All of these have given us scientific evidence of the civilisation that commenced in the fifth millennium BCE, as we know of it today, and continued without a break up to 1900 BCE.

This scientific evidence did not exist when the Britishers ruled India. They only made 'pronouncements'. Based on what? Linguistics, philology? These were purely statements by them so as to impose cultural dominance on Indians and take a higher pedestal for themselves. Quotes by them have proved their efforts at deliberate misinformation which was not based on any science or historical records. Regrettably, we took those pronouncements as gospel truth. Various types of post-partition evidence that included archaeological excavations, their reports of new findings which were aided by other sciences, papers written, etc. were all overlooked or were relegated to dustbin not only by the western scholars but also by those Indian historians and archaeologists who still stuck to the British view.

Despite all their efforts, it is my view that the British rulers failed to subvert Indian thought and culture. But what they could not do, a group of our Indian historians elected to carry forward their agenda. To this day, they persist with the view that was held by the British rulers.

The Britishers had no choice for the reasons mentioned earlier. They had to prove that Indian culture was not superior to theirs in the days when the empire was in its full glory and the 'sun never set on the Empire'.

What about our theorists. At least one can forgive the 'rulers'; they did not have the scientific evidences of archaeology, hydrology, astronomy, Carbon-14 dating, etc. India, of today, does have that. Are we not proud of our heritage?

But there is hope! After going through at least a dozen books that carried a mention of Aryans, I was delighted that their authors had started questioning the 'mainstream' view, a term used by the pro-believers of 'Aryan Invasion'. However, the protagonists dominated the National Council of Education Research and Training (NCERT) which publishes text books for schools and also dominated some of the institutes of higher learning. We should question the line of teaching. Here are some posers:

(a) Why was 'Arya' of the *Ṛigveda* converted to Aryans? Was it not known that 'Arya' signified the 'noble' and 'cultured' in the *Ṛigveda*?
(b) 'Arya' did not signify a race or a group of people speaking a common language. How does one account for terms 'Indo-Aryans' and 'European Aryans'?
(c) Max Müller said that Sanskrit, Greek and Latin (and some others) had a common ancestry. He hypothesised that it therefore was an Indo-European language. And since it was an Indo-European language, it had to have people speaking

that language. Where, then, was the home of Indo-European speakers?

(d) As a corollary, where is the home of Indo-Aryans. In about two centuries, the protagonists must have found that out!

(e) How does one explain the theory that Aryans arrived in 1500 BCE, but they invaded in 2000 BCE or earlier?

(f) How is it that if the Aryans wrote the *Ṛigveda* in 1200 BCE, they described the Sarasvati as 'mighty flowing river' when the river had dried up by 1900-2000 BCE?

(g) If the people were not invaders but immigrants who arrived around 1500 BCE and were dubbed as 'pastoral cattle breeders', how come they were able to spread and teach Sanskrit to a civilisation that spanned a million and a half square kilometres?

(h) How can one accept the fact that the 'pastoral cattle breeders' had the divine knowledge as also the capability to stipulate a ruling hierarchy to govern a state, a fact that is evident in the *Ṛigveda*.

(i) If the Vedas were composed in 1200 BCE, how do the Vedic gods appear in Mitanni treaty of the 14th century BCE?

To sum up. One must admit that ancient Indian history, based on scientific evidences, tells us that there was no Aryan invasion. There was no immigration from outside of the country either. There has been a continuity of a civilisation that commenced in the fifth millennium BCE at least (that is what we know of the vintage as of today) and continued till 1900-2000 BCE.

It is evident that the Ṛigvedic people were the authors of the Harappan Civilisation that existed in the Indus-Sarasvati valley as well as in Gujarat.

Notes

1. Voltaire, *Fragments historiques sur l'Inde* (first published Geneva:1773), in *OEuvres Completes* (Paris: Hachette, 1893), vol 29, p. 386.
2. Voltaire, *Lettres sur l'origine des sciences at sur celle des peoples de l' Asie* (first published 1777), letter of 15 December 1775.
3. Quoted by A.L.Wilson in *A Mythical Image: The Idea of India in German Romanticism* (Durham, N.C.: Duke University Press, 1964)
4. P. Sonnerat, *Voyage aux Indes orientales et a la Chine* (Paris: 1782), quoted in *Les Indes Florissantes-Anthologie des voyageurs francais* 1750-1820) by Guy Deleury (Paris: Robert Laffont, 1991), pp. 16-17.
5. Quoted by T.R.Trautmann, *Aryans and British India*, p. 112.
6. Friedrich von Schlegal, letter to Ludwig Tieck of 15 December 1803, quoted by Leon Poliakov in *The Aryan Myth*.
7. Dadabhai Nauroji, *Poverty and Un-British Rule in India* (London 1901, reprint New Delhi: Publications Division, Government of India, 1962, p. iii.
8. A. Anquetil-Duperron, *Legislation Orientale* (Amsterdam 1778), quoted in *Les Indes Florissantes, op cit.*, pp. xv-xvi.
9. William Digby, *'Prosperous' British India* (London: 1901), p. 141, quoted in "Golden Bengal", *The Modern Review*, (Calcutta), October 1908, pp. 298-99.
10. Brook Adams, *The Law of Civilisation and Decay* (London: 1900), quoted in "Golden Bengal", op.cit.
11. Voltaire, *Fragments historiques sur l'Inde, op.cit.*, p. 383.

12. F. Max Müller, *A History of Ancient Sanskrit Literature* (Allahabad: 1859, reprint New Delhi: Asian Educational Services, 1993), p. 17.
13. F. Max Müller, *India-What Can It Teach Us? op. cit.*, p. 71.
14. Ralph T. H. Griffith, from the preface to *The Hymns of Rigveda* (Delhi: Motilal Banarsidass, 1973), p. iv.
15. John Wilson, *India Three Thousand Years Ago*, quoted by Devendra Swarup in "Genesis of Aryan Race Theory and Its Application to Indian History" in *Aryan Problem*, eds. S.B. Deo and S. Kamath, pp. 33-35.
16. F. Max Müller, "On the relation of Bengali to the Arian and aboriginal languages of India", in *Report of the British Association for the Advancement of Science*, 1847, p. 349, quoted by T.R.Trautmann in *Aryans and the British India*, p. 176.
17. F. Max Müller, *My Autobiography, op. cit.*, pp. 311-12.

Further Reading

Agarwal, D.P. *The Indus Civilisation: An Interdisciplinary Perspective*. New Delhi: Aryan Books International.

Chakravarti, Dilip K. 2008. *The Battle for Ancient India*. New Delhi: Aryan Books International.

Danino, Michel.2000. *The Invasion That Never Was*. Delhi: Mother's Institute of Research and Mysore: Techprints.

Keyoner, J.M. 1998. *Ancient Cities of Indian Civilisation*. Karachi: Oxford University Press and American Institute of Pakistani Studies.

Lal, B.B. 1997. *The Earliest Civilisation of South Asia*. New Delhi: Aryan Books International.

—-. 1998. *India 19947-1997: New Light on Indus Civilisation*. New Delhi: Aryan Books International.

—-. 2002. *The Sarasvati Flows On: The Continuity of Indian Culture*. New Delhi: Aryan Books International.

—-. 2005. *The Homeland of the Aryans: Evidence of Rigvedic Flora and Fauna & Archaeology*. New Delhi: Aryan Books International.

—-. 2009. *How Deep are the Roots of Indian Civilisation: Archaeology Answers*. New Delhi: Aryan Books International.

Nath, Amarendra, et al. 2014. Site Catchment Analysis of the Harappan Site of Rakhigarhi, District Hissar. *Man and Environment* xxxix(1): 33-45.

—-. 2015. Harappan Internments at Rakhigarhi, Haryana. *Man and Environment*. (In press)

Rao, S.R. 1973. *Lothal and the Indus Civilisation*. Mumbai: Asia Publishing House.

Index

THE BOOK

This book is about the history and culture of India 5000 years ago. It aims at reaching out to the common man, from young students to grown-ups, who are not aware of the various discoveries brought forth through excavations since Independence.

To illustrate the point, students from 1950s onwards have not been taught about the discoveries in the field of archaeology and associated sciences, which have disproved the theory of Aryan Invasion. Therefore, they still say that the Aryans invaded India. As a corollary, they are learning that the Aryans threw out the Dravidians who, according to the Britishers, inhabited the Indus valley till the Aryans came. They still talk about it being the 'Indus Valley Civilization' despite the fact the 'centre of gravity' of this civilization was the Sarasvati valley.

The fault lies in our teaching system; reluctance to update the school books and books at university level which continue to 'parrot' the thinking of 1950s. The authorities that be need to accept the mass of professional papers, books and evidences of archaeology, anthropology, geology, archaeo-botany, etc. to set right our history which has been much maligned by the colonial rulers and their protégés that have ruled the Indian teaching systems.

Section I of the book deals extensively with the richness of the Indus-Sarasvati Civilization: its origin, growth and maturity, its town-planning, trade and commerce, artistic creations, etc.

Section II exposes the mind-set of the colonial rulers and their agenda to demean Indian civilization. Each one of their theories has been struck down, not in the least by Indian archaeologists but also by professionals all over the world. **This Section demonstrates in clear terms that the Vedic people were neither 'invaders' nor 'immigrants' but indigenous and they themselves were the authors of the Indus-Sarasvati Civilization**.

THE AUTHOR

Air Vice Marshal Rajesh Lal (Retd.), born 1948, was commissioned in the Indian Air Force in 1968 as a fighter pilot. He fought actively in the 1971 war with Pakistan and headed an operational base during the Kargil war. A qualified Flying Instructor, Production Test Pilot and a graduate of National Defence College, India, he commanded a front-line fighter squadron and two fighter bases. He held staff appointments at Command level, Air Headquarters level and at the Ministry of Defence.

After retirement in 2006, he completed his Commercial Pilot's Licence and was the Chief Pilot at the Indira Gandhi Rashtriya Udan Akademi. He retired from active flying at the age of 65 with about 8000 hours of flying experience.

His interest in archaeology developed when he started assisting his father, Professor B.B. Lal, Padma Bhushan and former Director General of Archaeological Survey of India, in proof-reading his books. With this new love, he hopes to publish a couple of more books on the richness of Indian culture.